THE
TRANSFORMATIONAL
LEADER

HOW TO BUILD A COMPETITIVE ADVANTAGE BY INSPIRING, MOTIVATING AND ENGAGING TEAMS IN TIMES OF INCREASING CHANGE.

ANTON VAN DER WALT

Cover design, internal design and editing: Lauren Shay – Full Stop Writing, Editing and Design.

CONTENTS

CONTENTS

CONTENTS

CONTENTS

ABOUT THE AUTHOR

Anton van der Walt is the author of *Leadership Through My Lens*, a book combining two of his passions: photography and leadership. He has spent 20 years working in corporate positions across the globe, including China, the Middle East, South Africa, Europe, Australia and Thailand.

"How people work with people" is the driving force behind a lot of Anton's thinking and teaching. He is passionate about inspiring people and guiding business leaders to best develop themselves, their teams and the business. He combines his years of personal experience, along with those of the many highly successful people he has worked with, to create tools and innovative techniques that inspire and motivate.

Anton firmly believes that great leaders are truly passionate about what they do. This passion brings out the best in those they lead.

Find out more at antonvanderwalt.com.

ANTON VAN DER WALT

PREFACE

It was in July 2017 that the idea behind this book was born. In the months leading up to July, I had arranged many leadership webinars, discussing self-awareness and the importance of self-management in a leadership development context. I focused on the significance of leadership influence, as opposed to leadership power, and how important it was for leaders to lead from the front with humility.

My passion lies in leadership development. I have conducted hundreds of leadership coaching and mentoring sessions over the years. Many of the leaders I have coached have been highly successful in their industries, and I was fortunate to interview a number of these leaders for this book. But more about that later.

My webinars during the early part of 2017 were well attended, and it became apparent I needed to expand on this subject as an author. At the time, it was all about disruption and how leaders needed to develop not only to cope, but also to thrive in a world of change and disruption.

I called on my good friend, Kristofer Kumfert. He helped me brainstorm and put together thoughts and ideas on how to spread the transformational leadership development message.

PREFACE

It was during this time I developed the Transformational Leader model: know yourself to lead yourself, to lead the team, to lead the business, and to lead the industry. I am forever grateful to Kris for the illuminating sessions we shared.

Once I had the Transformational Leader model in place, it gave me a clear direction on how to build the rest of this book. It took almost 12 months to complete. In creating the content, I researched traditional leadership theories, as well as contemporary thinking in the leadership field.

This book focuses on leadership transformation and growth, a subject on which much literature already exists. However, unlike many other texts, I have included valuable personal insights, case studies and stories from leaders who are not only surviving in a disruptive business world, but thriving.

With this idea in mind, I approached more than 400 executive leaders across the globe, inviting them to share their wisdom and stories on this subject. I interviewed leaders from the United States, Canada, Germany, England, Europe, Asia, the Middle East, South Africa and Australia. The most relevant insights and valuable pieces of wisdom from some of these executive leaders are included in this book. I am incredibly grateful for the time they afforded both me and you, the readers of this book.

The stories and ideas are varied, and it is clear that every leader has to walk their unique path. However, there are many common threads in their experiences. They understand the critical role of self-awareness – the ability of a leader to apply self-leadership and vision in terms of the future of leadership. Leaders at this level want to share their wisdom and experience and are only too happy to help. I saw this over and over again while interviewing these highly successful and very busy people, who went out of their way to make time to share their thoughts and ideas with me. The interviews are kept in their original format to retain the conversational style.

I do not expect anyone to read this book cover to cover in one sitting. It is a combination of textbook, workbook and inspirational read on transformational leadership. The reader is likely to focus on the portion of the book that relates to their particular needs at the time.

As a handbook/textbook, the models focus on the "why," "how," "what" and "what if" of leadership concepts and ideas. The content changes as the reader progresses through the stages of transformational leadership, but the model construction remains the same. It is important the reader sees this thread throughout the book.

The interviews with the executive leaders are strategically placed throughout the book. In many cases, the reader may find themselves drawn first to these personal accounts and pieces of wisdom for their valuable insights and inspiration.

Lastly, I am grateful to my two editors, Lianne Embleton and Lauren Shay, who worked through these concepts and ideas and helped me bring this book to life. Thank you, Lianne and Lauren!

THE WORLD YOU SEE AND THE LIFE YOU LIVE ARE YOUR CHOICE.

ANTON VAN DER WALT

TRANSFORMATIONAL LEADER MODEL

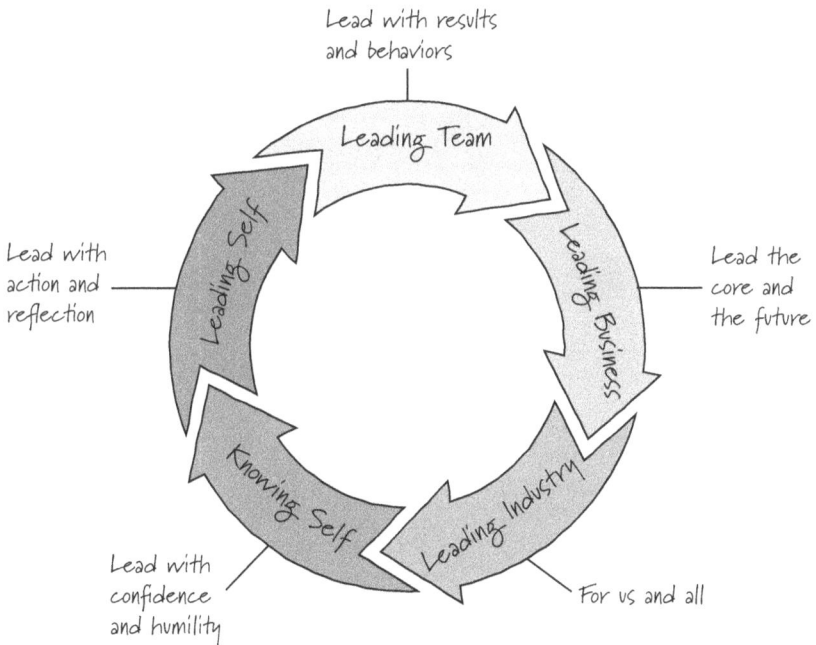

Lead with results and behaviors

Leading Team

Leading Self

Lead with action and reflection

Lead the core and the future

Leading Business

Leading Industry

Knowing Self

Lead with confidence and humility

For us and all

ANTON VAN DER WALT

INTRODUCTION

THE CASE FOR CHANGE

There is no question that occupying a senior executive or chief executive role is challenging. A *Harvard Business Review* article in May 2017 highlights a staggering statistic. From 2000 to 2013, almost 25% of Fortune 500 CEO departures were involuntary. This means that 25% of CEOs in this category were either dismissed or asked to leave their positions. According to the article, these forced departures had cost shareholders an estimated $112 billion in lost market value annually.[1]

The concerns of a senior executive are tremendous. These concerns typically fall into three key areas: the personal, the professional and the talent of their teams.

---

1 Elena Lytkina Botelho, Kim Rosenkoetter Powell, Stephen Kincaid and Dina Wang, "What sets successful CEOs apart," *Harvard Business Review*, May-June 2017. https://hbr.org/2017/05/what-sets-successful-ceos-apart

INTRODUCTION

1. PERSONAL

- They struggle to meet professional obligations while trying to live a balanced life.
- They feel overwhelmed by their to-do list. "What do I delegate? What can I stop doing? How do I carve out essential thinking time? How do I enjoy what I'm doing?"

2. PROFESSIONAL

- They ask themselves, "Is my leadership style agile enough and ready to adjust to the world of today and tomorrow?"
- They want to deliver results over the short term and set the business over the long term.
- They feel frustrated when their business model is disrupted by innovation.
- They need to revamp leadership development, focusing on "who" leaders are rather than "what" they do. They focus on business results and people.

3. TALENT

- They need to find, develop and keep the right tech-savvy talent.
- They seek ways to develop a cohesive, high-performance culture in their organization that embraces innovation, risks and opportunities.
- They strive to create and maintain a positive team-orientated culture that fosters trust.

"For me, success is one simple thing and it's the very essence of being a leader. It's building or having the ability to recognize talent and build that talent around you. You can talk about a million different leadership traits, but without this one key thing, you cannot succeed.

"If I look at one point, actually, I was managing across multiple countries. Now, I couldn't physically be in all these countries. I couldn't physically be on the ground in all these places at once, but by recognizing talent, surrounding myself with the right team, articulating them, I got things done. You could be the most enigmatic, charismatic, intelligent person in the world, but without the right people, you fail. It's plain and simple."

Dominic Keogh-Peters
Chartered FCIPD, Group HR Director, Axiom Telecom
United Arab Emirates

THE IMPACT OF SENIOR LEADERS GLOBALLY

The impact of senior leaders at a global level is valued in the billions of dollars. Therefore, it's critical that leaders inspire their teams to future-proof their organizations in disruptive industries.

The questions leaders must ask themselves are:

- How do I support my organization with change efforts?
- Do I inspire and engage my teams?

- Do I deliver transformation through culture and accountability?
- What stops me from achieving excellence?

LEADERSHIP REALITIES

Senior leaders are confronted with numerous leadership realities daily. They must deal with many competing priorities, such as:

- Acting and delivering with speed, urgency and decisiveness.
- Interpreting and visualizing the future, and engaging employees and key stakeholders.
- Having an adaptive mindset in a disruptive environment, with the ability to continually reposition the business.
- Leading from the front with humility.

Global leaders are also kept awake at night by critical challenges:

- Disruption is no longer simply a catchphrase – it's a reality.
- They don't know how to deal with this disruption.
- As organizations get flatter and information is more readily available, empowerment is increasingly critical to succession.

These elements democratize leadership at all levels of an organization.

"I originally was in hotel management years ago. My first management job, after my graduate traineeship, was as an events manager. I had a team of 12 people. I had a little fancy blazer, I worked for a large hotel group, I had a nice title on my business cards.

"In reality, I had to set up conference rooms. We turned the rooms around three times a day. Now, quite often, it would be two o'clock in the morning and we would have to set up a room for six o'clock in the morning. I learned that to get the job done, I had to be the first to pick up the Hoover and Hoover the floor to get the room ready. Then my team followed.

"As silly as it may sound, no one ever taught me that in a classroom. It's an extreme example but these days, I still lead a medium-size team for an HR department, but I will be the first to get something done or show people how to do something. That, for me, is critical leadership learning."

Dominic Keogh-Peters
Chartered FCIPD, Group HR Director, Axiom Telecom
United Arab Emirates

INTRODUCTION

"There are so many things that must keep executive leaders up at night. I don't envy them one bit. Their jobs are hard. One challenge that comes to mind is the impact of technology and figuring out how to pay for it.

"What do I mean by that? Right now, it seems easier for new and unproven companies to get a free pass on profitability and have access to money to make 'technology investments' than it is for a legacy company generating billions of dollars in revenue and profit to do the same to transform/disrupt their own business.

"I can't speak for executives, but what would keep me up at night wouldn't be knowing what to do, but instead trying to figure out how to pay for it without failing to meet Wall Street expectations, executing too slowly to stay relevant to customers or not getting my people to change. The burden of a legacy business is to maintain that cash machine while making investments to transform the business. The options appear to be either bite the bullet and risk the legacy business, or mortgage the future to fund new investments. To compound the issue, the ability to execute comes down to a reliance on leadership quality at all levels.

"What Jeff Bezos did with Amazon was amazing. He broke the mold on building a business and, fortunately, had an idea that, once accepted, disrupted businesses and generated huge returns. He didn't even make an annual profit until 2003. His company lost millions for a long time. Do you think a legacy business and its leaders would be given that kind of pass from Wall Street or its employees? The rules are different for large legacy companies and they stifle innovation. Honestly, it's not that large companies are any less innovative, they are just constrained by a different set of business, cultural and leadership rules.

"Imagine what would happen if a global company said, 'You know what? We're going to lose $30 billion over the next three years, but here's what we're going to do. We're going to plough that money back into the company and, in four years, this is what we expect to see.' There is no way in the risk-averse environment of legacy businesses that they take that risk. The Street would reject the idea, short the stock and destroy the business and its leaders. Employees would be worried about their jobs and retirement, and revolt rather than rally together. "Yet, that is what is required to drive innovation and disrupt the market. For them to be successful, leaders at all levels need to effectively lead their people through the unknown, get them involved in the solution, develop their talent to remain relevant, and help every employee see their place in the future."

John Hine
President, J. Hine Associates
Michigan, United States

CULTIVATING LEADERSHIP IN A DISRUPTIVE ENVIRONMENT AND A DISRUPTIVE WORLD

"Everyone thinks of changing the world, but no one thinks of changing himself."
– Leo Tolstoy

Given the rapid rate of disruption and emerging competitors, particularly in sectors previously protected by patents and high-entry cost, transformational leadership is essential to survival. For senior leaders to thrive in a disruptive environment, three critical components are required:

1. **Results.** Leaders who understand their environment deliver improved results. These include personal results, business results and people metrics.
2. **Accountability.** An individual and organizational culture of accountability transforms leadership. You and your team must be accountable. This means doing what you say you will do.
3. **Influence.** Leaders must move from a position of power (telling) to a position of influence (motivating).

"I've often seen CEOs using positional power when they're under stress. So, when they've got time, they're consultative and they're charismatic. But when they're stressed, they play the power card. And it's those clients who in difficult situations can remain true to themselves and true to the whole developing of people, being consultative, being inclusive, who succeed. To me, that's a big differentiating factor."

Henda Smit
CEO, The Makings, Industrial Psychologist
Johannesburg, South Africa

As a senior leader, it's essential you understand what drives you and what derails you. This understanding has great benefits for you and your organization. This is because any change in an organization is affected by the leader who looks inward and looks outward. This means learning to see obstacles as opportunities, rather than negatives to be avoided at all costs.

"After years of collaboration and efforts to advance the practice of leadership and cultural transformation, we've become convinced that organization change is inseparable from individual change. Simply put: change efforts often falter because individuals overlook the need to make fundamental changes in themselves."[2]

2 Nate Boaz and Erica Ariel Fox, "Change leader, change thyself," *McKinsey Quarterly*, March 2014. https://www.mckinsey.com/featured-insights/leadership/change-leader-change-thyself

MOVING FROM POWER TO INFLUENCE

In a business environment increasingly defined by disruption and the democratization of information and control, power through authority becomes ineffective. Change is needed, and it starts with the leaders themselves.

The critical shift is to move from a position of power to a leader of influence. Power through authority is about three things: it's position-based, it's ego-driven and it's directive or all-knowing. On the other hand, power through influence is person-based, collaborative and inspirational.

Understanding the difference between power and influence requires self-discovery. As a leader, you need to develop your strengths, which are equally as important for the organization. In fact, a study conducted by Gallup found that "strengths intervention" – implementing strengths-based management practices in companies – led to a 10%-19% increase in sales, 14%-29% increase in profit, 9%-15% increase in employee engagement and a 26-72-point decrease in employee turnover in high-turnover organizations.[3]

A willingness to change is key to survival. And change starts by looking inward. It starts with the self. There are three elements to creating change: self-awareness, engagement and transformation.

---

3 Brandon Rigoni, PhD., and Jim Asplund, "Developing Employees' Strengths Boosts Sales, Profit, and Engagement," *Harvard Business Review*, September 1, 2016. https://hbr.org/2016/09/developing-employees-strengths-boosts-sales-profit-and-engagement

"Very recently, I've had a lengthy conversation with one of the leaders exploring this concept of power in a group setting. If you want to be a leader, you need to have a source of power. The question is, what is your source of power? You need to feel powerful to be able to shake things up. You need to feel powerful to be able to challenge. You need to feel powerful to stand up for your values and set the right direction.

"But what is your source of power? That is a huge differentiating factor between a leader who can be successful in a sustainable manner and who's running a marathon, versus someone who's short-term and is running a sprint and cannot be successful sustainably.

"So, I go back to the source of power. For some people, the source of power is simply the purpose. I am so committed to the purpose that I just find the power. The purpose inspires me, so I have the power to do what I think is right. For some people, the source of power is their title, the position they have. They may not be respected, but it's just the sheer title and the position. I'm the boss, right? For some people, it's the relationship they have built, the trust their people have in them, the charisma they bring in. So, that gives them their power and people listen to them.

"For some people, it's just one-up – I'm the boss. I am empowered as a CEO, so I can do what I want and people will follow! Over time, one finds how shallow this source of power can be, as you have very few followers, people who follow out of fear.

INTRODUCTION

"Of all the many sources of power, purpose is the most powerful. A leader backed by the power of purpose stands to win in the longer term. A leader who is backed by the power of relationships, trust, values and mutual respect stands to win in the longer term.

"The ones who are tied to the title and position, the ones who are tied to the power from one-up, are the ones who don't have their own source of power and, hence, come across as being superficial and weak, although they like to feel that they're powerful. They are not, actually – that's why they fail to command the respect and followership, if I can use that word, the other kind of leaders get."

Kamali Rajesh
Head of Human Resources APAC, Syngenta Asia Pacific
Singapore

1. SELF-AWARENESS

Years ago, one of my mentors said to me, "There are two reasons why people change. They see the light (become aware), or they feel the heat." Self-awareness is a deliberate effort – it's not achieved overnight. It's a lifelong quest, and it's critical for three reasons. Firstly, self-awareness is a strong predictor of success. It is also a core ingredient of emotional intelligence. Secondly, it builds confidence and self-esteem. Thirdly, it requires introspection. It is about truthfully asking yourself the tough questions so you can modify your behavior.

2. ENGAGEMENT

Success is measured by delivering results, maintaining high standards and holding people accountable – including yourself. Engagement is key to this culture of success for three reasons. Firstly, leaders who engage with their teams and organizations remain "teachable", asking for and providing feedback. They lead by teaching others, rather than "telling". Secondly, a premium is placed on self and employee development. Thirdly, personal and organizational values are never compromised.

INTRODUCTION

"I recently met a leader from the Blanchard Group, and they've just completed a study on employee engagement. The research suggested the single biggest predictor of employee engagement and motivation was the ability of the leader to focus on others first rather than themselves; leaders who are genuinely interested and care about their team versus leaders who are self-centred, worrying about their own power, their own control, their own position.

"This resonated with me. We have all heard the saying that 'employees don't leave the company; they leave their boss'. Some people get to a senior position based purely on their ability to deliver but struggle to be good leaders and often have low emotional IQ.

"If I were to use a past example of a great leader, it would be Alan Mulally from Ford. Alan had an amazing sense of awareness of himself and others. His emotional IQ was off the charts. He was a truly authentic leader who everyone respected. He had all the traits of a great leader, but I think for me, his ability to connect is what set him apart as a leader."

Gayle Antony
General Manager, Head of Global Learning and Development,
Nissan Motor Company
Nashville, United States

3. TRANSFORMATION

Accountability is fundamental to successful transformation. It is what delivers a healthy, sustainable culture. Firstly, successful transformation takes place on two levels: within the individual and within the organization. Secondly, leaders who anticipate disruption and plan for it can successfully transform the organization. Thirdly, transformational leaders deliver change through culture and empowerment. Empowerment is what delivers accountability.

To grow or have influence, we require change. There are three levels of change: in others, in the organization and in the self. Firstly, others are the people you work with, the people you work for and the people working with you. You do not control who they are, how they turn up or how they go about doing what needs to be done. This you can only influence. Therefore, it is critical your influence is at an optimum level.

Secondly, change is needed in the way the organization functions. What is the culture, what results does it deliver and how sustainable is it? We cannot control these things as much as we would like. Again, it is about influence. Why? Because you need people to make an organizational change – you cannot do it yourself.

Thirdly, you need change in the self. This is you. You have full control of this level of change: what you think, what you say, and what you do. There is no influence required here. However, awareness and understanding are required: who you are, what motivates you, and what derails you.

It is really in the self-awareness stage where change starts. This is where the change is most impactful. Transformational leadership, therefore, begins with self-awareness. Transformational leadership means developing and growing leadership. And transformation means not simply taking a different approach; it means developing a whole new vision of your leadership.

THE FIVE STAGES OF TRANSFORMATION

There are five stages of transformational leadership:

1. **Know yourself.** This is self-awareness: who you are, what motivates you and what derails you.
2. **Lead yourself.** This is about self-management: taking care of yourself, self-control and mindfulness.
3. **Lead the team.** This is understanding team metrics, team effectiveness, deliverables and how the leader and individuals function in the team.
4. **Lead the business.** This is business and people metrics: strategy, culture and engagement.
5. **Lead the industry.** This is about courage, legacy and, most importantly, influence.

We will explore the five levels of transformational leadership in greater detail throughout the rest of this book.

WHAT IS TRANSFORMATIONAL LEADERSHIP?

Transformational leaders lead by example. They lead from the front and encourage, inspire and motivate followers towards their vision. Transformational leaders express a clear purpose, are passionate about what they do and stand for, and communicate a clear vision for themselves and their company.

These leaders are optimistic, energetic and enthusiastic, traits that are infectious. Transformational leaders encourage and inspire their teams to innovate and create change to shape the future success of the company. They challenge employees to go beyond the ordinary, to create an aspirational future, one that once may have seemed impossible.

WHAT DO THE BEST TRANSFORMATIONAL LEADERS DO?

A study conducted by the *Harvard Business Review* on S&P 500 and Global 500 firms in 2017 found that stories of successful transformational and change efforts were exceptionally rare.[4] However, the study discovered that most successful transformational leaders and companies shared the following five common characteristics and strategies:

1. THEY ARE NOT ALWAYS INSIDERS

Jeff Bezos, founder and CEO of Amazon, came from the world of finance, while Reed Hastings, CEO of Netflix, had a background in software. This meant these two leaders had no predetermined way of doing things in their companies, which turned out to be a great asset for them.

---

4 Scott D. Anthony and Evan I. Schwartz, "What the Best Transformational Leaders Do," *Harvard Business Review*, May 8, 2017. https://hbr.org/2017/05/what-the-best-transformational-leaders-do

2. THEY STRATEGICALLY PURSUE TWO SEPARATE JOURNEYS

One of the biggest reasons why transformation fails is because companies follow an inflexible, singular approach, trying to build a new company from an old one. Success requires repositioning the core business while actively investing in the new-growth business.

Apple is probably the best example of this approach, through the launch of its iMac and iBook on the one hand and iPod and iTunes on the other. Reinvigorating the core Macintosh franchise and launching a new device and content through iPod and iTunes became a significant growth opportunity for Apple.

3. THEY USE CULTURE CHANGE TO INCREASE ENGAGEMENT

Satya Nadella, CEO of Microsoft, is often credited with transforming Microsoft's cautious, insular culture into one of risk-taking and empowerment. Nadella, a hands-on engineer, built his reputation not as a visionary, but as someone with a keen ability to listen and learn. Rather than making speeches to engage and motivate employees, he favoured company-wide "hackathons", empowering employees to work on projects they were passionate about.

4. THEY SHARE POWERFUL NARRATIVES ABOUT THE FUTURE

Mark Bartolini, chairman and CEO of Aetna, challenged the company to transform its classic health insurance business model into one that engaged much more deeply with its members and their personal health goals.

For the culture to change and the business to move into new growth areas, Bartolini said the CEO needed to become "the storyteller in chief".

"The CEO's responsibility is to create a stark reality of what the future holds, and then to build the plans for the organization to meet those realities," he said. The result was that Aetna's value-based healthcare, as a new growth opportunity, accounted for 40% of total revenue in 2017.

5. THEY CREATE A CLEAR ROADMAP BEFORE DISRUPTION TAKES HOLD

Transformation typically takes years and often won't be completed during the tenure of a CEO. Many well-known disrupted companies, such as Kodak, Blockbuster and Blackberry, ran into trouble years after the first warning signs appeared. None of their leaders developed effective transformation plans in time to halt the decline.

In stark contrast was Netflix, for instance. Netflix CEO and chairman Reed Hastings realized as far back as 2007 that the company needed to take the leap from DVDs to online movie and TV streaming. Now, Netflix has more than 139 million streaming subscribers worldwide.

TRANSFORMATIONAL LEADER: A CASE STUDY

The situation. A global multinational CEO in the auto industry was struggling. His span of control included total operations, manufacturing, multiple plants, product development, finance, marketing and sales, including service and parts, as well as other support functions such as legal, government affairs and human resources. The company was a significant player in the industry and a long-established business.

The person. The person was an expat in a foreign country. He was a smart guy, but his host culture was vastly different from his home culture. He was in a highly pressurized position. Visibility was high, both internally and externally. He had many competing priorities and not enough time to deal with them all. The initial shock was overwhelming. The team did not gel, the results were indifferent and there was a lack of accountability. He told me, "I cannot understand this. Where I come from, when you ask someone to do something, it happens. Here, I have to double-check everything. I'm the CEO. Why do they not just do the things I tell them to do?"

The employees. The employees perceived the CEO as aloof. They believed he didn't care about them, provided no support or feedback, and was only concerned about delivery. They said, "He does not know us. He could not care about our culture; it is just about power and the results. Just another expat. We will wait till he leaves."

The solution. To become a transformational leader, the CEO needed to concentrate on two areas. Firstly, he needed to immerse himself in the culture of the country and the company. He needed to understand what made people tick – what was important to them and what motivated them? I told him, "While you seem to be the same, you are not. They don't see you as one of them. As such, you'll never get the best out of them if you don't change." I also said, "You first need to connect with your people before you can teach them anything. If they don't accept you and have respect for you, they won't follow you." Secondly, he needed to look in the mirror. How did he turn up, how did he behave and what did he say? In other words, how did people experience him? He said to me, "I'm not aloof. I really care what happens to these people. I desperately want to help the organization and the people become world-class and sustainable."

He had two choices. He could either see the light (the obvious) or feel the heat. This organization was worth billions of dollars, so failure was not an option. Fortunately, he saw the light and went down the road of self-discovery. He realized that connecting with people was more about the people and less about himself. He realized what behaviors brought success and what behaviors derailed him.

What happened next? There was a significant change in the organization, not only in terms of business but also in people metrics. His proactive demeanor became infectious. His direct report team started working smarter and stopped waiting for his instructions. His influence became apparent, having a marked influence down the organization's line. It was clear the CEO and his team had moved from a position of power (telling) to a position of influence. Hard measurables, such as profit targets, customer satisfaction targets and employee engagement targets, showed significant improvement. It became obvious that the leadership team was setting the pace and culture on "how people should work with people". They became the leaders others wanted to follow.

There were, of course, individuals who did not like this new environment. They liked it better when they could play the victim. That way, they had excuses. In the end, some did not last in the company – the heat became too intense for them.

How did this play out over the medium term? As the business grew, the company's share in the country's market grew. Not only did customer perceptions change, but employees also became proud and protective of their company. The company became an aspirational employer, meaning the quality of graduates and other prospective employees increased significantly. It became much easier to find the right candidates, even if the organization was not a "millennial-type" company. The CEO said to me, "I love this place and the people. I get so much done here. I have never worked in a place where I've felt like there are people who will do absolutely anything for me and the company."

And the future? As the market share grew, so did the company's reputation. It provided a platform for the CEO to participate in industry and government policy frameworks. It also allowed the company to set the future of the industry.

THE EYES THROUGH WHICH YOU SEE THE WORLD DETERMINE THE SHAPE OF YOUR WORLD.

KNOWING SELF (SELF-AWARENESS)

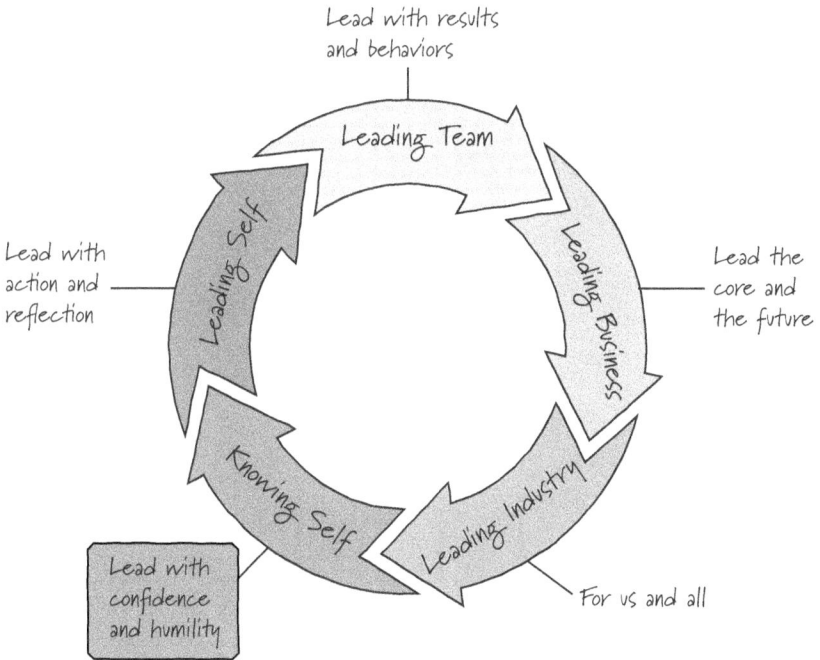

Lead with results and behaviors

Leading Team

Leading Business

Leading Self

Knowing Self

Leading Industry

Lead with action and reflection

Lead the core and the future

Lead with confidence and humility

For us and all

PART 1

KNOWING SELF (SELF-AWARENESS): LEAD WITH CONFIDENCE AND HUMILITY

WHAT IS SELF-AWARENESS?

Self-awareness is being conscious of one's character and emotions. It's an understanding of what drives you and what derails you. It means paying attention to what you do, how you do it and why you do it.

Self-awareness is a skill. It's not always easy to be consciously aware of your weaknesses, strengths and behaviors. To become a transformational leader, it's critical you have a thorough understanding of the thoughts, feelings and relationships you share with your tribe, community and fellow employees.

"I do think one thing about this new, upcoming generation is they need to be able to think for themselves more. I do believe this whole issue around core values is critical for people to think about.

"Who are you as a young leader? What really drives you? Does what you're driven by match what the organization you're working for is driven by? If yes, then you're in the right place, and if no, then you should look for a different place to spend your energy and time and earn your money.

"I think complacency has no place in leadership. It's not a leadership behavior that anyone should seek to develop."

David Everhart
Senior Vice President, Leaders & Talents, Mannaz A/S
London, United Kingdom

STRATEGIC PERSPECTIVE: SELF-AWARENESS

RELATIONSHIP MODEL SUPPORTING SELF-AWARENESS

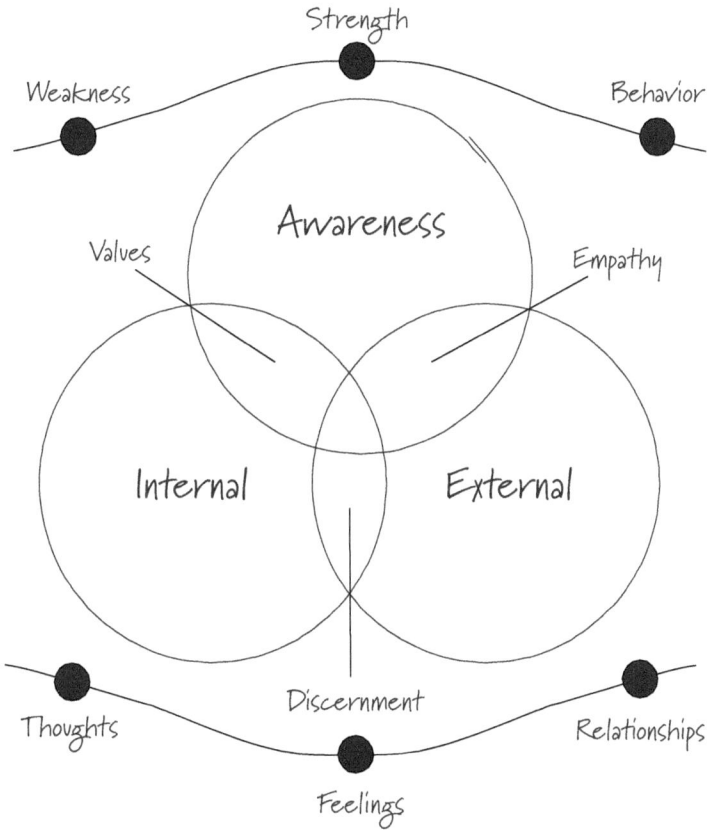

Strength

Weakness

Behavior

Awareness

Values

Empathy

Internal

External

Thoughts

Discernment

Relationships

Feelings

PART 1: KNOWING SELF (SELF-AWARENESS)

"From my experience, leadership is about being and not doing. Being in the flow, being yourself. Being aware of where you're coming from and what influences the way you show up as a leader every single day. Just be. This isn't about chasing something all the time; this is about being there. To me, this understanding is very powerful.

"There are times that I felt the first one (doing as opposed to being) was more important. But as I age and as I grow, and as I see other leaders, I see the latter is more powerful. The more you are able to do the second piece, the first piece sorts itself out. So, to me, leadership is more being rather than doing."

Kamali Rajesh
Head of Human Resources, APAC, Syngenta Asia Pacific
Singapore

To gain a strategic perspective of self-awareness, let's look at the three core components:

1. **Awareness.** The conscious recognition and realization of one's weaknesses, strengths and behaviors. It is an understanding of what behaviors derail and what behaviors propel.
2. **Internal.** This refers to our values and passions and how we execute them. It incorporates our personal preferences and emotional intelligence.
3. **External.** An understanding of how others see us and experience us, and the impact we have on their lives.

At the three intersections are:

1. **Values.** These are part of our belief system. They have a major influence on our behaviors and attitude towards the self, others and society.
2. **Empathy.** This is about figuratively "standing in another person's shoes". It's the ability to understand or share another's feelings and emotions.
3. **Discernment.** This refers to our ability to make a balanced call or judgment of a person or situation. We discern and measure others according to our value system.

The impact of self-awareness on the ability to lead effectively cannot be understated. In fact, studies show that self-aware leaders create more satisfied teams and profitable businesses. Researchers found there are two broad types of self-awareness: internal and external. *Internal self-awareness* is how accurately we recognize our values, passions, aspirations and reactions, and how these impact others. High internal self-awareness is associated with higher job and relationship satisfaction, personal and social control, and happiness. On the other hand, *external self-awareness* is our understanding of how others view us. People who have an accurate insight into how others see them tend to be more empathetic.[1]

This means leaders who see themselves as their employees do tend to have a better relationship with their teams. In turn, employees feel more satisfied with their leaders and see them as being more effective. Unfortunately, there are many factors that can impede a leader's self-awareness.

---

1 Tasha Eurich, "What Self-Awareness Really Is (and How to Cultivate It)," *Harvard Business Review*, January 4, 2018. https://hbr.org/2018/01/what-self-awareness-really-is-and-how-to-cultivate-it

"I think the great leaders are definitely curious in the sense that they are constantly focused on their own learning and development. And that, I think, naturally rubs off on how they lead. So, curiosity would be one aspect.

"The great ones really, genuinely care about people. They really do. And I don't think they can fake that.

"The other one, I think, is that they really are focused on winning, and I mean that in a good way in terms of the team winning. I think people like to win. People like to be successful. They really do.

"The great leaders, they know that it's a three-legged stool, if you will, in terms of being curious and always learning, and making people feel loved and making them feel successful. I think the great ones do those three things."

Kris Kumfert
Chief Human Resources Officer, Clark Pacific
United States

OUR REALITY

- We are in a rapidly changing and challenging world. Technology and communication advances have caused our world to shrink. We instantly know what is happening around the world at any point in time. We are continually bombarded with new information.

- To cope with this information overload, we must constantly adjust, adapt and change – at work and in our personal lives. But we cannot simply make external adjustments; they must come from within.

- Change is not always comfortable. This means we lull ourselves into thinking and believing things will not change. This is a mistake that sets us up to fail. Things will change, and if we are not ready or unable to accept or adjust to change, we set ourselves up for disaster.

- Rather than be proactive about change, too often we remain outwardly focused. We believe our lives are subject to luck, chance or fate. It is easier to believe that events and other people are responsible for our successes or failures. This puts us firmly in a position of having no control over our lives, where we blame events and others for our situation.

- At some point, we must realize that blaming others for our situation is not helpful. We cannot change others; we can only change ourselves. We must turn our focus inwards and have a good look at our thoughts, attitudes and behaviors. We must be conscious of how we manage our lives.

PART 1: KNOWING SELF (SELF-AWARENESS)

- The eyes through which we look at the world determine what we see. Perception and perspective affect the way we perceive the world. Depending on our perspective, the world will be negative or positive.

- Therefore, it is crucial we effectively manage the self to effectively manage and understand the world around us.

STUFF HAPPENS

The jackass penguin of Southern Africa is known for its donkey-like bray. The Stony Point penguin colony is found in Betty's Bay, on South Africa's Overberg coastline, about 90 kilometres from Cape Town. This is one of only three such land-based colonies in South Africa. The colony first began in 1982 with the arrival of a breeding pair of penguins, presumably from nearby Dyer Island. The colony has since grown to include about 150 breeding pairs.

I take great pleasure in watching the way their comical waddle on land becomes a highly efficient diving and swimming skill the moment they enter the water. One day, a certain individual stood out in the crowd of relatively clean penguins. It appeared to be covered in what I could only imagine was bird "poop". I had a bit of a chuckle as he certainly seemed disgruntled about this noticeable flaw in his appearance.

This got me thinking about the saying "stuff happens". Sometimes, bad things happen seemingly for no reason. Things go wrong. They may be totally unexpected and random. Stuff happens, and this is an undeniable fact of life.

The best way to cope when this happens is to do the following:

- **Acceptance.** Accept it has happened and move on. If we do not get out of denial, nothing will change. Recognize and reorganize.

- **Change.** Change the situation. One cannot hope the problem will go away. Find alternatives and deal with the situation. Be proactive – there is no use remaining a victim.
- **Intuition.** Trust your instinct. We know when we must do what we need to do. We know what the answer is. Trust yourself and follow your gut instinct. Your intuition is designed to ensure your survival.

With hindsight, we understand there is a reason and purpose for everything that happens to us. Deep down, we know the difficulty we are experiencing is there to teach us something. The sooner we can see its purpose and accept it, the sooner we can move on.

WHO AM I? WHAT SHAPED ME?

The fact we have difficulty accepting change or responsibility for our lives relates to our inability to effectively manage ourselves. Many factors shape who we are and how we react to change and adversity. To manage ourselves, we must ask the following:

- Who am I? Where am I?
- What makes me the person I am?
- What are the reasons for me being here?
- How best can I achieve what I need to achieve?

Our lives are partly shaped by what we have inherited from our parents (our personality and character) and the environment we have been exposed to. Our lives are the sum of all our acquired knowledge, experiences and skills.

It is true that you may have been exposed to powerful influences beyond your control during the early, impressionable stages of life. Growing up in a society where prejudice is tolerated or even encouraged, or where parents were unable to provide the love and support needed by their young children, can have a profound and long-lasting effect. We tend to become what we have been taught early in our lives. Much of this learning has no basis in truth but is largely seated in emotion.

The emotional content of these early impressions conditions us. This conditioning lies within our unconscious mind and is part of our belief system. We often experience these positive or negative impressions as our current reality. The conditioned impressions create blockages that lead to certain behaviors, attitudes, values and motives. When we are confronted with a stressful event, we may find we have a predisposed response. This type of response is often negative and almost always based on fear – in particular, the fear of change or loss of self-identity, relationships and possessions.

These predispositions influence our self-image, as well as the way we see others. They affect how we present ourselves and how we behave in certain situations. To create change and maximize our potential, we must modify these potential stumbling blocks. A new mindset is required. Personal growth does not mean you need to become someone different. It is about discovering your strengths and developing your potential – becoming the person you are meant to be.

It is a choice we make. It is a choice you can make this instant!

PART 1: KNOWING SELF (SELF-AWARENESS)

"Nobody is going to be successful as a leader unless they have that inner drive, that motor. That thing that gets them out of bed and inspires them to motor on to bigger and greater things. I've reflected on that myself because I come from a very humble background. But from an early age, I was driven to improve, driven by a belief that there was a bigger and better world out there. And that translated into academic success, sporting success and university success in those early years.

"So, by the time I was 18, I already had pulled myself up from nowhere to get myself into a position of the strong personal belief that I could achieve more in this world and move away from the economically and industrially depressed east end of Glasgow, and go carve a career around the world.

"The first thing I'm trying to get to here is that what's driven me as a leader throughout all my many years of experience is a sense of passion. That emotion. That drive. That engine of fire that lies within you. Without that, I don't think you can possibly be a leader.

"And curiously, when I speak to young people, I find a lot of people don't have that inner motor. They don't have that fire. They don't have the ambition. Maybe they've been raised too easily. I don't know why they don't have that mindset, but I realized, if I didn't have that, I wouldn't be where I am today.

"The second important thing is that normally, leaders cannot be successful without the contribution of others.

This empathy for others, this ability to inspire and lead other people around you, is key to every leader's success. There's no leader out there who started on his own, and there's no leader who can be successful unless they have that special empathy, that ability to deal with all walks of life – both internally, in terms of inspiring them for better things, and also externally, the multiple stakeholders we have to deal with.

"And I think that's been the key to my success. I've dealt with presidents in many different countries at that level. And I've dealt with the lowest of the low in any organization and found I've been able to develop synergy, a vocabulary of common sense of spirit with them. And in my organization, I've got 71 different nationalities and I have to be able to communicate with all of them. I think a leader who has that ability to adjust his vocabulary in the pantomime of life is absolutely vital.

"Don't feel you're so big that you can never go down to those individual people who have made whatever sacrifice, whatever contribution. Be sure to stop and recognize that.

"You can't be a successful leader unless you've got that inner passion, that drive, and empathy with all sorts of people from all different levels, internally and externally. These, for me, have been two key points of a successful leader."

David Greer, OBE, FIMechE CEO, Serco Middle East, Africa and India, and Executive Committee Member of Serco Group

INTRODUCTION TO PSYCHOMETRIC ASSESSMENTS

Achieving permanent change in your leadership is within reach. But it requires an understanding of who you truly are. It also requires you to take control of your life. Psychometric assessments are the cornerstone of gaining this self-awareness.

The Institute of Psychometric Coaching defines psychometric assessments as: "A standard and scientific method used to measure individuals' mental capabilities and behavioral style. Psychometric tests are designed to measure candidates' suitability for a role based on the required personality characteristics and aptitude (or cognitive abilities). They identify the extent to which candidates' personality and cognitive abilities match those required to perform the role."[2]

In turn, self-awareness is the ability to reflect on these assessed behaviors and characteristics, and the impact they have on others. For this reason, there is a direct correlation between self-awareness, individual effectiveness and managerial excellence.

THE CORE OF SELF-AWARENESS IS EMOTIONAL INTELLIGENCE

Our emotions push us to take action. They are indispensable in our everyday lives. We can act irrationally, or we can recognize and understand our emotions and act intelligently.

---

2 "Introduction to psychometric tests," Institute of Psychometric Coaching. https://www. psychometricinstitute.com.au/Psychometric-Guide/Introduction_to_Psychometric_Tests. html

Emotional Intelligence (EQ) provides us with a set of skills that enable us to recognize and manage our emotions. When we have high EQ, we have the ability to not only recognize our emotions and feelings, but also the feelings and emotions of those around us.

Dr Travis Bradberry, the co-author of *Emotional Intelligence 2.0*, says EQ is the ability to recognize and understand your feelings and the feelings of others and to influence those feelings to your advantage.[3]

Author and EQ expert Daniel Goleman says that EQ combines four capability elements.[4] The first is self-awareness, the ability to understand your feelings and behaviors. The second is self-management. The third is social awareness or reading the emotions of others. And the fourth element is relationship management or social skill. Understanding your behavior and others' behavior enables you to build stronger relationships with the important people in your life.

Each capability element has a specific set of competencies, as listed below:

3 Travis Bradberry and Jean Greaves. *Emotional Intelligence 2.0: Discover How to Increase Your EQ.* 2009.

4 Daniel Goleman. "Leadership That Gets Results," *Harvard Business Review*, March-April 2000. https://hbr.org/2000/03/leadership-that-gets-results

PART 1: KNOWING SELF (SELF-AWARENESS)

SELF-AWARENESS	SELF-MANAGEMENT	SOCIAL AWARENESS	SOCIAL SKILL
Emotional self-awareness: The ability to read and understand your emotions, as well as recognize their impact on work performance and relationships. **Accurate self-assessment:** A realistic evaluation of your strengths and limitations. **Self-confidence:** A strong and positive sense of self-worth.	**Self-control:** The ability to keep disruptive emotions and impulses under control. **Trustworthiness:** A consistent display of honesty and integrity. **Conscient-iousness:** The ability to manage yourself and your responsibilities. **Adaptability:** Ability to adjust to changing situations and overcome obstacles. **Achievement orientation:** The drive to meet an internal standard of excellence. **Initiative:** A readiness to seize opportunities.	**Empathy:** Sensing other people's emotions, understanding their perspective and taking an active interest in their concerns. **Organizational awareness:** The ability to read the currents of organizational life, build decision networks, and navigate politics. **Service orientation:** The ability to recognize and meet customers' needs.	**Visionary leadership:** Ability to take charge and inspire with a compelling vision. **Influence:** Ability to wield a range of persuasive tactics. **Developing others:** The ability to bolster others' abilities through feedback and guidance. **Communication:** Listening and sending clear, well-tuned messages. **Change catalyst:** Proficient at initiating new ideas and leading people in a new direction. **Conflict management:** The ability to de-escalate disagreements and orchestrate resolutions. **Building bonds:** Cultivating and maintaining a web of relationships. **Teamwork and collaboration:** Competent at promoting cooperation and building teams.

In summary, EQ is perhaps the most critical factor in leading a fulfilled life. Compared to IQ, it is a better predictor of academic success, job performance and life success. And, unlike IQ, we can increase our emotional intelligence throughout life.[5]

UNDERSTANDING LEADER DERAILERS

Being self-aware is the conscious recognition and realization of your weaknesses, strengths and behaviors. Understanding what behaviors derail you is critical to leadership success.

A derailer is a behavior that impedes progress. It is a weakness that requires improvement. Examples of derailers include an inability to change, a lack of trust, low emotional intelligence and inability to deliver results.

5 Daniel Goleman. *Emotional Intelligence: Why It Can Matter More Than IQ*. Bloomsbury Publishing: 1995.

PART 1: KNOWING SELF (SELF-AWARENESS)

"I think the answer to that question (what are a leader's derailers?) depends on perspectives. If I ask an employee about my leadership and what my derailers are, I think their answer will be different than if I ask my boss.

"For example, a mid-level manager in a multinational firm trying to climb the ladder is likely to be caught up in the politics of dancing. They have placed career over service to their people and customers and, therefore, are focused inward rather than leading. To my manager, who may also aspire to climb the ladder, I may be viewed as highly successful and highly effective. To my people, I'm likely absent and viewed as incompetent and ineffective. Depending on the politics and culture of the organization, those two perspectives can both be correct.

"Now, if that same manager bucks the system and says, 'Well, I don't worry about politics and career. What I'm really focused on are developing my people and the efficiencies and effectiveness of my department,' then politics don't matter. As a result, there is potential that my boss may view me as ineffective, but my people may view me as highly effective as I create change and support and work on their behalf.

"I think the question is a really, really good one. I can think of numerous cases of organizations where both of these perspectives are true, and I've observed and experienced the outcomes of both. One creates roadblocks for a leader going forward but their people love them. The other – they get promoted but they're less competent to lead. Yes, they've done a great job of serving their individual aspirations but left behind a wake of damage and done little to prepare the next generation for leadership.

"Maybe this is why we still spend resources on leadership development. Maybe today's leaders haven't been groomed properly by their predecessors in how to lead. Maybe those before them didn't set a good enough example and shifted the focus somehow to movement and the importance of relationships in getting stuff done. Maybe we've moved away from process execution in management to leveraging relationships, i.e. politics, and become distracted from focusing on our teams, leading by example and improving employee capabilities through coaching and feedback. Show me a company that says it gets things done through relationships and I'll bet it has low engagement scores (as a result of misguided leadership) deep in the organization."

Well, how do you define success?

"In the perfect world, it would be defined using the company vision, mission, values and the achievement of business objectives. To simplify this discussion, let's focus on team capabilities, the ability to exceed customer expectations and financial results. If, as a manager, you're not growing your people, making improvements in your department, and engaging your team in finding solutions to customer problems, you're not an effective leader. If a leader's focus isn't on trying to make employees' and customers' lives better and improve the business, I'm not sure what they are doing. Your sole purpose as a leader should be to build your team's capabilities to operate without you and make your department so efficient that it doesn't need managing; in essence, putting yourself out of a job.

"As leaders, we become ineffective when we lose sight of what matters. What really matters isn't what we decide matters, it's what our customers and people decide matters. Maintaining that perspective may help defend against more self-promoting and politically oriented behavior.

"If leaders act in a self-serving manner, feel threatened by growing the capability of their subordinates, lose sight of the customer and don't focus on business execution, they become derailed. Customer satisfaction, engagement and business results become the priorities and measures of success, not individual agendas, i.e. getting promoted."

John Hine
President, J. Hine Associates
Michigan, United States

WHAT DOES IT MEAN WHEN A LEADER DERAILS?

A derailed leader has failed to reach expectations. One report describes derailing as: "When a manager who was expected to go higher in the organization and who was judged to have the ability to do so is fired, demoted or plateaued below expected levels of achievement."[6]

A report published by Hogan Assessments says popular literature contains many examples of derailed leaders. "Dixon's (1976) book, *On the Psychology of Military Incompetence*, provides heartbreaking accounts of military disasters caused by incompetent leadership. Finkelstein's (2003) review of business failures contains stories less tragic than Dixon's accounts, but reveals many of the same themes."[7]

Indeed, in his book, *Why Smart Executives Fail: And What You Can Learn From Their Mistakes*, Sydney Finkelstein lists "the seven habits of spectacularly unsuccessful people":

1. They overestimate their strength and underestimate the strength of the competition.
2. They put personal interests ahead of company interests.
3. They are arrogant and make reckless decisions.
4. They eliminate anyone who challenges their decisions.
5. They ignore operations while trying to manage their company's image.

---

6 M. Lombardo and C. McCauley, "The dynamics of management derailment," Center for Creative Leadership, Greensboro, NC, 1988).

7 Joyce Hogan, Robert Hogan and Robert B. Kaiser, "Management Derailment: Personality Assessment and Mitigation," Hogan, 2009.

PART 1: KNOWING SELF (SELF-AWARENESS)

6. They minimize difficult obstacles and don't plan accordingly.
7. They rely on outdated strategies and tactics.

So, rather than a flawed business strategy, it is often "poor execution, defined as not getting things done, being indecisive, not delivering on commitments" – in other words, leader derailment – that leads to business failure.[8]

---

8 Ram Charan and Geoffrey Colvin, "Why CEOs Fail," *Fortune Magazine*, June 21, 1999. http://archive.fortune.com/magazines/fortune/fortune_archive/1999/06/21/261696/index.htm

"I've worked in every continent, as it happens, and the one thing that I've seen as a major factor in derailing people is a lack of cultural sensitivity. I think the inability to adapt to different cultures can be a serious barrier, whether you're dealing with Arabs, whether you're dealing with Russians, whether you're dealing with Americans. Cultural sensitivity and the ability to adapt to that culture is absolutely key.

"I think the other thing that derails people is the inability to listen and to even believe that other people may have an alternative point of view. It may not be a better point of view than yours, but it is an alternative that is worthy of consideration. And I've seen all too often, people attack certain methods, where it's my way or the highway, who don't take time to stop, look and listen to what others might have to say. I think everyone's got a contribution in that regard.

"The third thing I would say is that some people, and I've been guilty of this myself in the past, is I'm a very fast thinker, in that if I see a problem, I can come to a solution rapidly. And while it makes eminent sense to me that is the right way to go, you learn very quickly that sometimes you have to walk slow to go fast, because in going through your thought process, while you have zoomed through the steps in your own mind, some people haven't even left the starting blocks. I learned that early in my executive career, about 35. I've always been conscious of that, that no matter how quick you can see an answer, you must give others the time to mature the idea in their own mind and get comfortable that it is indeed the right solution.

"So, a lesson for me is, you think you're carrying the team, but very often it's useful just to stop, look and listen to make sure they have indeed caught up with your thought process so that you can have a team-winning solution rather than an individual solution. I know that by deliberately taking the time to get people on side with you, at the end of the day, the whole ship will get to the destination, and not just the skipper. Everyone will come with you and celebrate collectively on that success. And it's paid off. It's paid off quite a bit, actually."

David Greer, OBE, FIMechE CEO, Serco Middle East, Africa and India, and Executive Committee Member of Serco Group

FOLLOW-THROUGH: THE ROADMAP TO INSIGHT IN SELF-AWARENESS AND LEADER DERAILERS

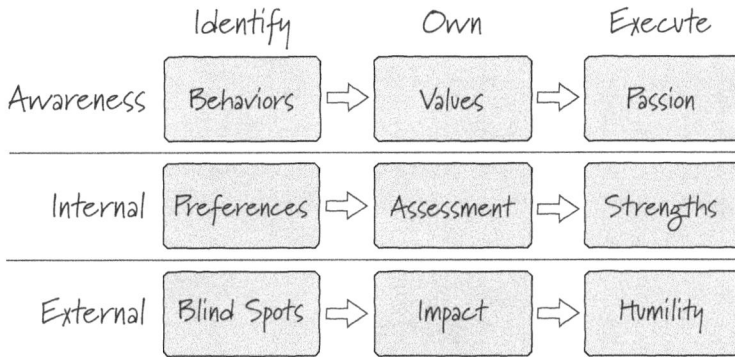

	Identify		Own		Execute
Awareness	Behaviors	⇨	Values	⇨	Passion
Internal	Preferences	⇨	Assessment	⇨	Strengths
External	Blind Spots	⇨	Impact	⇨	Humility

To avoid derailment, leaders need insight. Insight means putting the nine strategic components of self-awareness to work. This is done through a process of **identification**, **ownership** and **execution**.

AWARENESS

1. IDENTIFY YOUR BEHAVIORS

Behaviors relate to your actions, the things you do with and around others. They also relate to how others experience you. Understanding psychometric assessments gives you an insight into why you behave the way you do. Behaviors manifest in three ways:

- **Style.** How you come across, how others experience you.
- **Conduct.** What you do and say.
- **Presence.** How you make others feel when you are in their space and how you affect their emotions.

PART 1: KNOWING SELF (SELF-AWARENESS)

"I think the biggest derailer that I have seen in leaders is their habit to see the world only through their eyes. This also translates as the leader's inability to listen, see and sense what the team and the external environment is sending as signals.

"So, your inability to adapt and listen to your team, to listen to your surroundings, what's going on, is the biggest derailer. Once you stop listening, it's only a matter of time, maybe a couple of years, until the organization will see it but the team sees it first and you fail as a leader.

"And that then brings me to the question of what's the fundamental value I look for in a leader when I look at hiring or my direct reports. I look at people who are willing to listen, who are willing to learn and can adapt to changes. Skills I can take care of over a period of time, but if they don't have these three fundamental traits displayed in their previous roles, I'll have challenges hiring them because I don't see them going ahead in their leadership journey."

Chhitiz Kumar
CEO, Philips Capital, Middle East and Turkey
United Arab Emirates

2. OWN YOUR VALUES

Values are part of a belief system. They have a significant influence on your behavior and attitude towards yourself, others and society. Values are:

- Standards you set for yourself. They are what you believe to be right or wrong. They also allow you to evaluate your behaviors and performance.
- They are based deep within your conscience and keep you awake at night if you abandon them.
- They function as a set of ideals you aspire to.

3. EXECUTE YOUR PASSION

When you live your passion, when you make decisions from a position of power that's based on passion, you experience joy, pleasure, happiness and satisfaction. It feels right and comfortable – you feel fulfilled.

Passion is about:

- **Joy.** You experience pleasure and happiness when you do what you are passionate about.
- **Being true to your nature and character.** This is the essence of your spirit – what makes you feel alive.
- **Your heart.** When you work on the things you are passionate about, you feel it deep inside. You know it is right.

PART 1: KNOWING SELF (SELF-AWARENESS)

"I believe people really are in control of their own careers. We have choices. In my case, I could have chosen to stay, which I was strongly encouraged to do by many people. They said, 'This will pass. You should just wait. Stay in position and in six months, a year, 18 months from now, this situation or this person will be gone.'

"For me personally, I wasn't willing to do that. I felt like, 'No, I'm not willing to be derailed or go into this eddy that somebody else has put me in and spin over there by the shore for a year and wait for that person to get out of the way so I can go back into the mainstream and continue progressing.' But that's a personal choice.

"I also believe most people, professional people, have a lot more choice than they think they do. Yes, I can be derailed by others; that's always going to be true. Also, I'm an at-will employee. I decided to join this organization for some reason at some point, and I could decide to leave and join a different organization. But most people don't do this. People are scared. I think one derailer for people is inertia caused by, 'I can't afford to leave my job.' There are many reasons why people decide not to leave a job, even though they should. I have watched and worked with people who were a wrong fit, sometimes for an entire career. They're unhappy, maybe successful, but unhappy in a career with an organization because they were unwilling or didn't think they had the ability to leave and do something different.

"Personally, I don't buy that. You have to make sacrifices or be willing to accept consequences – loss of income for some time, or maybe a permanent lowering of your income over 20 years, because what you're doing doesn't fulfil the purpose you feel is important."

David Everhart
Senior Vice President, Leaders & Talents, Mannaz A/S
London, United Kingdom

INTERNAL AWARENESS

4. IDENTIFY YOUR PREFERENCES

Preferences are your preferred way of operating and are identified in psychometric assessments. When you operate in your preferred state, executing work comes easy because you are functioning at an optimal level. Operating according to your preferences means:

- You don't have to expend a lot of energy to deliver a particular result.
- Preferences are your "go-to" behaviors – your natural or impulse behaviors. For example, if your preference is to analyze detail before making a decision, processing a large amount of data would come easily to you. Alternatively, if your preference is to look at the "big picture", having to process large amounts of data would drain you.
- Preferences are where you feel the most comfortable. In other words, they are your bias.

PART 1: KNOWING SELF (SELF-AWARENESS)

5. OWN YOUR RESULTS

Your psychometric assessment results are *yours*. They are the precise and factual outcome of what you answered about yourself. This is not someone else's opinion of you – it is your own.

Depending on your willingness to accept the results, you may or may not allow for growth. Growth will primarily depend on:

- Your **reaction** to the results. Do you accept or do you deny and question the results?
- Your **acceptance** of the results. This will open the door for new learning and growth.
- Acceptance of the **consequences** of the results. Acceptance of the consequences places you in a position of strength and knowledge. Once you are aware of what drives you and what derails you, you can adjust your behavior accordingly.

6. EXECUTE YOUR STRENGTHS

Assessment results allow you to identify your weaknesses and strengths. There is a good argument that you must place more focus on developing your strengths rather than being fixated on your weaknesses. To enhance your strengths, you must:

- Live with **conviction**. Live with a strong belief that you own your strengths and understand what weaknesses you need to work on.
- Have the courage to **accept** who you are – your true self.
- **Execute** your strengths to build your efficacy.

CONTRAST PROVIDES CLARITY

On a typically hot and rainy African afternoon, I took a boat ride along the Chobe River. The Chobe River flows along the extreme north-eastern border of Chobe National Park in northern Botswana. The park has one of the largest concentrations of game in Africa. The river is a major watering spot for large breeding herds of elephants, as well as families of giraffe, sable and Cape buffalo.

It was on this late afternoon cruise that we came close to several elephants drinking water on the banks of the river. I took some close-up shots of these magnificent creatures as they ambled towards us. The contrast of the golden sunlight as it bathed the elephants and the dark storm clouds on the distant horizon was beautiful. The contrast in the light made the elephants appear much larger and sharper in focus. In photographic terms, contrast refers to the relative difference between the light and dark areas of the print.

Practically speaking, contrast means the obvious difference between two or more things.

It is through contrast that we attain clarity. Esther Hicks, an inspirational American speaker, says: "Contrast allows you to know that which you do not want. By knowing what you do not want, you get to ask for what you do want."

Contrast, in life, gives us the opportunity to look at opposites. We cannot have cold if there is no hot, nothing can be tall if something else is not short, there is no pleasure if there is no pain. This is the irony of life. Only through the experience of one can we appreciate the other.

Role-model leadership gives us the opportunity to observe and model our behavior on the examples we aspire to. In contrast, we may find ourselves with a role model with whom we have no affinity. This is just as important, as it provides us with a contrast – knowing what we do not want makes knowing what we do want so much clearer.

As author John Steinbeck wrote, "What good is the warmth of summer, without the cold of winter, to give it sweetness." Understanding what we do not want is as important as understanding what we do want. Contrast provides us with clarity to understand the difference.

EXTERNAL AWARENESS

7. IDENTIFY YOUR BLIND SPOTS

A blind spot is a behavior or characteristic you are not aware of but is obvious to others. The Johari window, developed by Joseph Luft and Harry Ingram in 1955, is a useful psychological model that gives individuals an enhanced understanding of themselves and how are they perceived by others. The model is comprised of four quadrants, or "window panes", that signify thoughts, feelings and motivation, and whether this information is known or unknown to the self. In essence, it uncovers your blind spots, which can:

- Highlight a weakness that is unknown to you. This weakness could become a block to your growth and development
- Reveal an opportunity to develop remedial behaviors.
- Identify the risks if these behaviors are not addressed.

8. OWN YOUR IMPACT

How we treat others and what we do and say has an impact on ourselves, our team and the business. It's critical you develop an understanding of your impact on others. To do this, you must:

- Be comfortable asking for feedback. Ask people how you make them feel. What should you do more of and what would they prefer you stop doing?
- Know that other people make assumptions about you. Their assumptions are their reality, as much as your assumptions about others are your reality.
- You cannot control others' perceptions and opinions of you. You can only change your behavior and hope it has a positive effect.

OWN YOUR IMPACT ON OTHERS

Long-exposure photography has skyrocketed in popularity the past couple of years, with much coverage in landscape photography magazines and on photo-sharing websites. This is partly because so many different camera filters are now available. But it is mostly because of the beauty this genre captures – especially long-exposure night photography.

Blurred skies streaked with clouds, smoothed-out water creating flow, city-scape night photography and star and light trails are just a few of the incredible effects created by deliberately prolonged exposure time.

The futuristic skyline of ultra-modern Dubai offers a wonderful opportunity to use this technique. Recently, I tried this technique on a particularly clear night. I chose a position where I had a great view of the skyline, set my camera on a tripod and pre-set the exposure to 25 seconds. I hoped the wind would remain calm and no other movement would spoil the photo. The beauty and clarity of the photo were amazing.

This made me think about the difference just 25 seconds can make in our lives. If one can create something of beauty in 25 seconds, the opposite must also be true. It only takes a few seconds to admonish a person, break their self-confidence or verbally hurt them, causing long-lasting damage or irreversible harm. In those same 25 seconds, you could love someone, uplift them and give them constructive and inspiring feedback.

So, be mindful of what you do, say and think:

- **Pause before you speak.** Many of us speak first and think later. We may say things we regret. Pause to think – it gives you precious seconds to say the right thing.
- **Think before you write.** How many of us receive an email or message we don't like, get upset and shoot off a response, only to regret the content afterwards? This happens on social media all the time. People have even destroyed their own brand by making comments they later utterly regretted. I have never forgotten this good advice, given to me some years ago: "Sleep on it because tomorrow you'll have a much better answer, or maybe even no answer is all that is required."
- **Think about how you would feel.** Speak and write with empathy. Put yourself in the recipient's shoes. How would you feel receiving this comment or note? Would you feel happy or would it hurt?

Twenty-five seconds is all it takes. What did you do with your 25 seconds today? Did you help or did you hurt?

9. EXECUTE HUMILITY

Humility carries no pride, no sense of ego. It is an awareness of your shortcomings and the gracious acceptance that you are no better or superior to anyone else. Humility is when you:

- Show **empathy** towards others. You try to understand what they are going through.
- Are **respectful** of others' opinions. They have the same rights as you.
- Are **considerate**. Everyone has issues – often, they are unspoken.

THE IMPACT

Successful execution of the nine self-awareness components produces tangible benefits. It has a profound impact on your ability to grow self-awareness. Furthermore, understanding what may derail you (your weaknesses) and what propels you (your strengths) has tremendous benefits.

Remember:

- Transformational leadership starts with self-awareness.
- Transformational leadership means developing and growing leadership.
- Transformation means not simply taking a different approach; it involves developing a new vision of your leadership.
- Self-awareness requires deliberate effort and is not achieved overnight. It is a life-long quest.

The impact of becoming self-aware leads to the following:

Unaware	Aware
Limitations ✗	Freedom ✓
Ignorant ✗	Enlightened ✓
Indifference ✗	Compassion ✓
Apathy ✗	Empathy ✓
Detached ✗	Passion ✓

PART 1: KNOWING SELF (SELF-AWARENESS)

"I think the first and foremost important point is that leaders must always pay attention to culture. Culture is the main thing that drives a company towards being successful or not. It's the little habits that any leader should observe in terms of whether 'it's good or bad', and managing to get the best of those habits and also eliminating the bad habits in the company. That's something very important, in my opinion.

"The second thing as a leader, of course, is being close to your team and breaking barriers. They have to break the barriers and become a good listener because a lot of the time, leaders presume they are good listeners, but in reality, they do not allow space for listening when their people talk. So, allowing this space to be a great listener is something very important.

"The last thing is to be brave and be somebody who can really make tough decisions. When you reach into leadership, it's very important to really focus on the big picture. You need to be able to accept within yourself that there will be a lot of decisions you cannot make on consensus – you will have to make them for the sake of the big picture.

"If I may elaborate here, nobody, for example, likes to 'let people go' in a company. It's not something that anyone would enjoy, actually. Especially when you start thinking about their families and how it could affect them and their lives. But then again, you need to think about how making such decisions can help redirect the company in the right direction, build the right culture and, of course, help it succeed.

"Leaders need to be brave, in my opinion, to make some tough decisions that might help the company succeed.

"A lot of people might tell you, 'You know what? It's not really a traditional decision,' or, 'It's not really a decision that's going to help us grow,' and nobody sees that but yourself. It takes a lot of bravery for that leader to go ahead and do it with all the potential resistance yet make it happen and succeed."

Hisham Albahar
Chief Executive Officer, Posta Plus
United Arab Emirates

PART 1: KNOWING SELF (SELF-AWARENESS)

PREPARE YOURSELF –
WHEN THE NEXT DOOR
OPENS, YOU WILL BE
READY TO STEP INTO
A NEW AND EXCITING
SPACE IN YOUR LIFE.

LEADING SELF (SELF-MANAGEMENT)

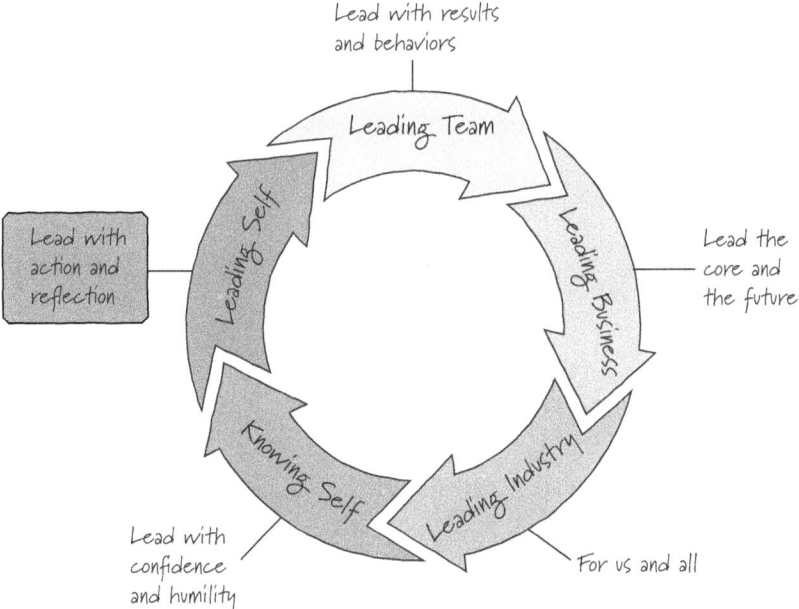

Lead with results and behaviors

Leading Team

Lead with action and reflection

Leading Self

Leading Business

Lead the core and the future

Knowing Self

Leading Industry

Lead with confidence and humility

For us and all

PART 2

LEADING SELF (SELF-MANAGEMENT): LEAD WITH ACTION AND REFLECTION

WHAT IS SELF-MANAGEMENT?

As indicated in the previous chapter, transformational leadership starts with being self-aware. It is also true that if we cannot "manage ourselves", how can we effectively lead and manage others? This is why self-management is a cornerstone to transforming oneself and will impact your ability to lead transformation.

Self-management means taking responsibility for who you are and how you behave. Certain behaviors and actions are required to effectively manage work and life. Self-management requires a certain skill set and the ability to apply certain techniques and tools. Insight into those aspects of work and life that pose the greatest challenges to self-management is critical.

STRATEGIC PERSPECTIVE: LEADING SELF (SELF-MANAGEMENT)

RELATIONSHIP MODEL SUPPORTING SELF-MANAGEMENT

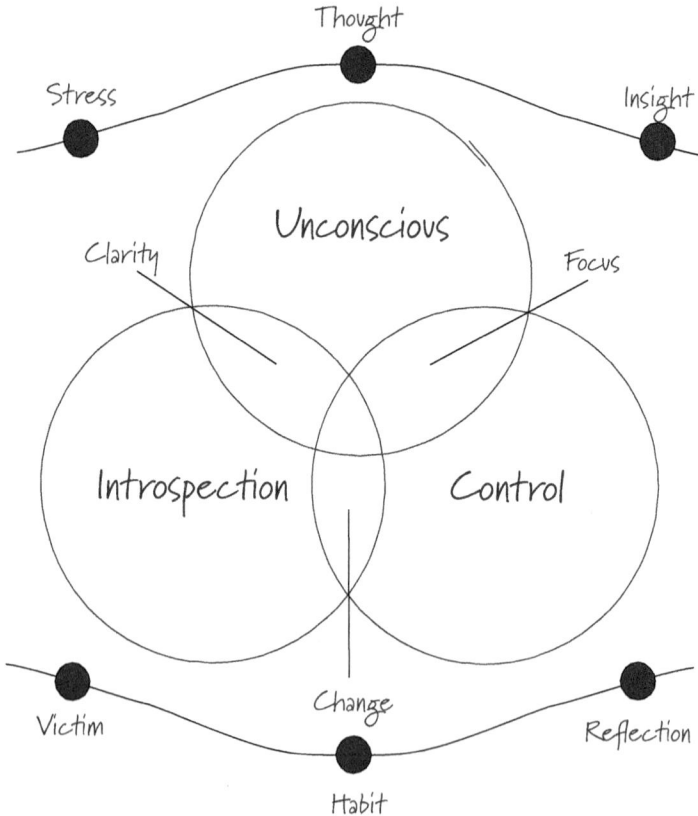

To gain a full understanding of self-management, let's look at its three core components:

1. **Unconscious.** According to psychoanalyst and neurologist Sigmund Freud (1856-1939), the unconscious mind is comprised of mental processes inaccessible to consciousness, but which influence our judgments, feelings and behavior. The unconscious mind is the primary source of human behavior. Like an iceberg, the most important part of the mind is the part you cannot see.
2. **Introspection.** This is the ability to observe one's own mental and emotional state of mind. It is understanding how and what you think and why.
3. **Control.** What we think, say and do is within our control, as are our emotions. We decide how we want to feel, how we turn up and how people experience us. The issues over which we have little, if any, control include current economic and political conditions and the opinions and behaviors of others.

At the three intersections are:

1. **Clarity.** Reflecting on one's feelings, emotions and behaviors provides clarity. Finding clarity of thoughts and actions helps us understand why we do what we do and the impact thereof.
2. **Focus.** Understanding what we can and cannot control provides a focus for our development. When we accept and focus on what we can control, we are able to remove blame.
3. **Change.** In accepting who we are and identifying our thoughts, feelings and behaviors, we can actively change and progress our self-development.

WE ARE BEING CHALLENGED

Not all changes present us with problems, but it is true that change causes of much of our stress. New situations, new relationships and unforeseen events can challenge our ability to cope and self-manage in our personal lives and as leaders.

It's important to remember that opportunities can emerge from every negative or traumatic situation, provided we exercise our privilege of choice. As previously discussed, depending on our perception of the event we are faced with, our response will have either a positive or negative outcome.

But the fact is, we learn and grow the most in situations of crisis and adversity. We are "forced" to react in a crisis. Although at the time we may not see the benefit, we do learn and grow from the experience.

In a leadership role, as in other areas of our lives, our natural response to a challenge is flight, freeze or fight. These responses are usually ineffective and do not provide us with the ability to learn and grow. It's important you take the time to appraise each challenge and decide on the appropriate way to deal with it. This means moving out of your comfort zone, where you blame others and external factors for the state of your life. Take responsibility and set new goals to begin your journey towards personal growth.

You *can* plan your future. You will spend the rest of your life in the future, so you may as well plan it carefully – starting now! It's only once we help ourselves become the person we are meant to be that we can begin to help others fulfil their potential, which is what transformational leadership is all about.

But first, we need to understand stress, the role it plays in our lives and how we respond to it.

THE COST OF WORKPLACE STRESS

Workplace stress and the experience of stress in general are often the biggest challenges to effective self-management. How we handle and manage stress has a profound effect on our ability to lead.

As a leader, what keeps you awake at night? Leaders face countless challenges. To cope, you must have resilience and the ability to handle and manage stress effectively. Why? Not only for your own well-being but because job stress can cost a business dearly. In fact, according to the American Institute of Stress, the cost of stress for US industry is estimated at more than $300 billion annually.[1] Management of stress, therefore, is crucial to effective self-management, productivity and leadership transformation.

THE PERSONAL COST OF STRESS

Stress permeates all levels of our consciousness: physical, psychological and spiritual. It touches every aspect of our lives and can upset our well-being.

Most people believe they can't do anything about preventing stress. Instead, they devise coping mechanisms and ways to control it. They may even say they need to be stressed to be competitive and survive in today's world. Nothing could be further from the truth!

---

1 "Transforming stress through awareness, education and collaboration," The American Institute of Stress. https://www.stress.org/workplace-stress/

PART 2: LEADING SELF (SELF-MANAGEMENT)

We know there are physiological aspects of stress that, if ongoing, may cause our bodies and minds harm. We also know there is a strong body-mind-disease connection. If stress is not proactively managed, we become exposed to a stress-causes-stress situation and our bodies suffer. Can we minimize the negative effects of stress by changing our attitudes towards it?

STRESS AND STRESSORS ARE EVERYWHERE

External stress is everywhere. Relationships at home and work cause stress. Fluctuating global markets and political developments also cause stress, despite being beyond our control.

Compounding the problem is that many people now operate on a 24/7 basis. Smartphones have changed everything – they are a blessing and a curse. On the one hand, you have the world in your pocket, but on the other, you are never far from your work, so it's hard to switch off. Employees are provided with mobile tools, such as tablets, laptops and smartphones, so their company can access them at any point in time. How many of us wake in the morning and the first thing we do is check our messages? What state of mind does this create?

Being constantly switched on leads to:

- **Stress.** We feel a general state of unease and anxiety, of not being in control. We wake each day with negative feelings and thoughts, fearing what the new day will bring.
- **Becoming a victim.** It is easy to blame something or someone else when you believe issues are beyond your control. It becomes a coping mechanism that prevents your growth and development as a leader.

- **Feeling under pressure.** We are under constant pressure to deliver. High demands are placed on us despite our limited ability to cope with them. There is no respite – one issue follows the next, demanding immediate resolution.
- **Anticipation of the unexpected.** The anticipation of random stressful situations is a vicious cycle: it creates more stress. Not knowing what will happen or what difficult issue we must deal with next results in extreme feelings of anxiety.

It's critical you realize that stress isn't merely a buzzword or an excuse: it is a very real physiological response to pressure and challenging situations.

PART 2: LEADING SELF (SELF-MANAGEMENT)

"I think one of the fundamental leadership challenges of our day that we haven't solved is information. How do we manage the tsunami of data and information that's coming across our virtual desks every day? To me, we've spent the last 20 years tearing down barriers to communication and tearing down barriers to access information, and now we live in this world where we have almost instantaneous access to information.

"If I want the answer to a question, almost any question I can think of, I can get some kind of answer. It may be biased; it may not be complete. It may be tailored in a way by someone who wants me to buy something from them, but I can get an answer to almost any question instantly. Anyone can send me an email, a chat. At a busy place like Ford or other companies, executives probably average 200 to 300 emails a day. How can any person possibly manage that amount of information?

"We need filter systems. We used to have executive assistants. Things just moved more slowly, so we could process them. Not an existential threat, maybe, to leadership, but a huge challenge right now is, 'How do we put back in place, or put in place, new ways of filtering all this data so we can make sense of it?' Because right now, I think people are trying to make sense of all the data.

"There's an expectation that senior leaders will be able to deal with this completely unrealistic amount of data that's coming to them every day, to the point where most executives I know can't take vacations anymore because of the thought of, 'Coming back from five working days where I didn't look at my email, suddenly I've got 1,000 emails that I haven't looked at in my inbox. It's too stressful and I can't relax.' I think we've created this world where we're a victim of our own technological success and we haven't figured out how to solve this. I'm convinced we will figure it out, but right now, I think those filtering systems are really not very good.

"It's almost like we also live in the age of plastics. Five hundred years from now, this will be the plastics era, where the world went through this addiction to plastic that lasted 150 years, and then we filled our oceans and created all these problems. Technologically, we solved that problem; it's already happening now – biodegradable plastics, or Coca-Cola bottles that are made of 80% biodegradable materials. That problem, I'm convinced, we'll solve over time, but right now, we're in the middle of it.

"I think the information problem is like that. We're in the middle of it. We don't know how to deal with this information. We have all these sources, and we are almost subconsciously driven by those sources. Somebody else is deciding what information we look at based on our behaviors and that, to me, is a bit scary."

David Everhart
Senior Vice President, Leaders & Talents, Mannaz A/S
London, United Kingdom

UNDERSTANDING STRESS: BIOLOGICAL EXPLANATION

Endocrinologist Hans Selye (1907-1982) is internationally acknowledged as "the father of the stress field". He pioneered the idea of the General Adaptation Syndrome (GAS), which he first wrote about in the British journal *Nature* in 1936.

GAS, also known as "the stress syndrome", is the process through which the body confronts stress. Selye explained that in GAS, the body passes through three universal stages of coping:

- **Stage 1: Alarm Reaction.** This is where the body prepares itself for a "fight-or-flight" response.
- **State 2: Stage of Resistance (or Adaption).** Provided the organism survives the first stage, it builds a resistance to the stress. The body adapts to the stressor it is exposed to.
- **Stage 3: Stage of Exhaustion.** If the duration of the stress is long enough, the body enters a stage of exhaustion. The body's ability to resist disease is significantly reduced or even eliminated.

Selye defined stress as the "mutual actions of forces that take place across any section of the body, physical or psychological". He argued that stress or stressing agents "could be anything from prolonged food deprivation to the injection of a foreign substance into the body, to a good muscular workout; by 'stress', he did not mean only 'nervous stress', but the 'non-specific response of the body to any demand'."[2]

---

2 "Hans Selye: The Discovery of Stress," Brain Connection. https://brainconnection.brainhq.com/2013/04/05/hans-selye-the-discovery-of-stress/

THE SYNDROME OF "JUST BEING SICK"

During his career, Selye revisited a theory he had begun to formulate when he was at medical school. He recalled that many patients had "felt and looked ill". They had "a coated tongue, complained of more or less diffuse aches and pains in the joints, and of intestinal disturbances with loss of appetite". They also "had fever, enlarged spleen or liver, inflamed tonsils, a skin rash," amongst other general symptoms.[3]

Selye devoted his life to the discovery of the cause of this non-specific illness. He believed there was some mechanism in the body that responded to external agents in a general way. The quality of "just being sick", which he had seen in those patients at medical school, suggested that "specific illnesses, if not wholly caused by a single influence, were certainly bound by similar forces; there was a link in the body's reaction to illness that gave the appearance of some internal mechanism combating the stressing agents."[4]

THE HYPOTHALAMUS-PITUITARY-ADRENAL SYSTEM

Through extensive research, Selye identified this complicated internal stress-processing mechanism. It became known as the hypothalamus-pituitary-adrenal system.

This system governs the amount and kind of response the body produces to combat a stressing agent. "Simplified, the

---

3 "Hans Selye: The Discovery of Stress," Brain Connection. https://brainconnection.brainhq.com/2013/04/05/hans-selye-the-discovery-of-stress/

4 Ibid.

hypothalamus (the bridge between the brain and endocrine system) sends a message to the pituitary gland (a hormone-producing gland embedded in bones at the base of the skull) to release ACTH (adrenocorticotrophic hormone) into the bloodstream. This signal prompts the adrenal cortex (located above the kidneys) to create corticoids, another hormone, from available raw material. These corticoids are then dispersed to the places in the body they are needed, where they are put to use in the various stages of defense against a stressing agent."[5]

Selye concluded that external outside stressors, such as physical pain, exposure to heat or cold and starvation, would create the same stress response every time. Stress is now viewed as "bad", as it is accompanied by a range of harmful biochemical and long-term effects that have rarely been observed in positive situations.[6]

FIGHT OR FLIGHT?

Early research on stress, conducted by American physiologist Walter Cannon in the early 1900s, established the existence of the well-known "fight-or-flight" response. This is a physiological reaction triggered by a quick release of hormones when a person experiences a shock or perceives a threat in their environment. The term "fight or flight" represents the two choices our ancient ancestors had when faced with danger: they could either fight or flee.[7] In fact, the fight or flight response is recognized as the first stage of Selye's GAS.

---

5 "Hans Selye: The Discovery of Stress," Brain Connection. https://brainconnection.brainhq.com/2013/04/05/hans-selye-the-discovery-of-stress/

6 Jayantee Saha. *Management and Organizational Behaviour*, New Delhi: Excel Books, 2006.

7 Kendra Cherry, "How the Fight or Flight Response Works", VeryWellMind, June 11, 2018. https://www.verywellmind.com/what-is-the-fight-or-flight-response-2795194

Cannon traced these reactions to the release of powerful neurotransmitters – chemicals that carry messages to and from the nerves – from a part of the adrenal gland called the medulla. The adrenal medulla secretes two neurotransmitters, epinephrine (also called adrenaline) and norepinephrine (noradrenaline), in response to stress. The release of these neurotransmitters leads to the physiological effects seen in the fight-or-flight response, e.g. a rapid heart rate, increased alertness, faster breathing.

It's important to note that the fight-or-flight response can be triggered by real or perceived threats – including in the workplace. When we are in this state of mobilization for survival for a prolonged period, it has negative consequences: we become excitable, anxious, jumpy and irritable. This dramatically reduces our ability to work effectively with other people and make good decisions.[8]

In the short term, we need to keep this fight-or-flight response under control to be effective in our daily lives and as leaders. In the long term, we need to keep it under control to avoid poor health and burnout.

8 Joseph Nii Abekar Mensah, PhD. *Stress Management and Your Health*, Strategic Book Publishing & Rights Agency, June 2013.

MANIFESTATIONS OF STRESS

It is generally accepted that prolonged stress can manifest in the following physical, emotional and psychological ways:

PHYSICAL MANIFESTATIONS	EMOTIONAL MANIFESTATIONS	PSYCHOLOGICAL MANIFESTATIONS
• Headaches • Colitis • Insomnia • Irritable bowel syndrome • Chest pain • Lack of energy • Sweating • Rapid pulse • Heart palpitations • Ulcers • Fatigue • Indigestion • Hypertension • Irregular menstrual cycles • Irregular pulse • Flushing • Sweating • Increased susceptibility to infection	• Irritability • Worry • Anxiety • Anger • Mood swings • Apathy • Depression • Impatience • Denial • Changes in dependency needs	• Memory loss • Fears • Withdrawal • Inability to concentrate • Panic attacks • Crying • Sleeplessness • Addictions • Compulsive behaviors • Disillusionment • Nightmares • Eating disorders • Loss of motivation • Depression • Phobias • Disintegration of daily routines • Forgetfulness • Disorganization • Substance abuse

STRESS AND IMBALANCE

Deepak Chopra, Indian-American author, public speaker and alternative medicine advocate, says aging is marked by a loss of many of the body's key balance points. Seniors often find their balance of blood-sugar levels, hormone levels and metabolic rate impaired.

One of the worst imbalances is high blood pressure. Hypertension is not a disease but a skewed cycle in the body's natural rhythm. Blood pressure is controlled by the brain, rising and falling during the day and responding to inner and outer cues. Blood pressure rises and falls in everyone, but for some people it does not return to its former level. Elevated blood pressure creeps in and, over time, the cyclic swing becomes skewed towards hypertension. The list of influences that raise blood pressure is long and wide-ranging. When the body is worked hard, blood pressure rises.

Emotional stress and anxiety can cause the same result. Even without any apparent outside influences, 90% of hypertensives have raised blood pressure with no identifiable cause for their condition. Researchers have tried to understand this situation by monitoring the blood pressure of different people with normal blood pressure, such as secretaries, nurses and stockbrokers. They found that during the day, specific events could cause blood pressure to rise, such as the secretary being scolded or the nurse treating a gunshot wound. Interestingly, several hours after the incident, their blood pressure levels had still not returned to normal.[9]

---

9 Deepak Chopra, *Ageless Body, Timeless Mind*, Great Britain: Rider, 1993.

PART 2: LEADING SELF (SELF-MANAGEMENT)

Chopra makes an important point here: "The body's memory of stress causes normal cycles to be thrown out of balance. Instead of returning to their original position, they drift slightly. Over time, the net result is a dynamic imbalance."[10]

The best defense against a perceived stressful situation is to preserve and renew the body's instinct for balance. Doctors previously believed that because blood pressure was controlled by the (involuntary) nervous system, it was beyond conscious control, but many years of research have shown that biofeedback, meditation, hypnosis and other mind-body techniques can control involuntary functions.

Chopra continues in this regard: "There is a very broad-based cycle in the body that directly reflects the aging process, the cycle of hormones. These messenger molecules carry an enormous amount of the information circulating inside us. If the hormonal balance can be preserved, we will have a reliable indicator that the flow of intelligence is also balanced. It is likely that many of the most important age changes are mediated by hormones triggered by stress and can be prevented by controlling stress."[11]

---

10 Deepak Chopra, *Ageless Body, Timeless Mind,* Great Britain: Rider, 1993.

11 Ibid.

STRESS: A CLASSICAL SYSTEMIC APPROACH

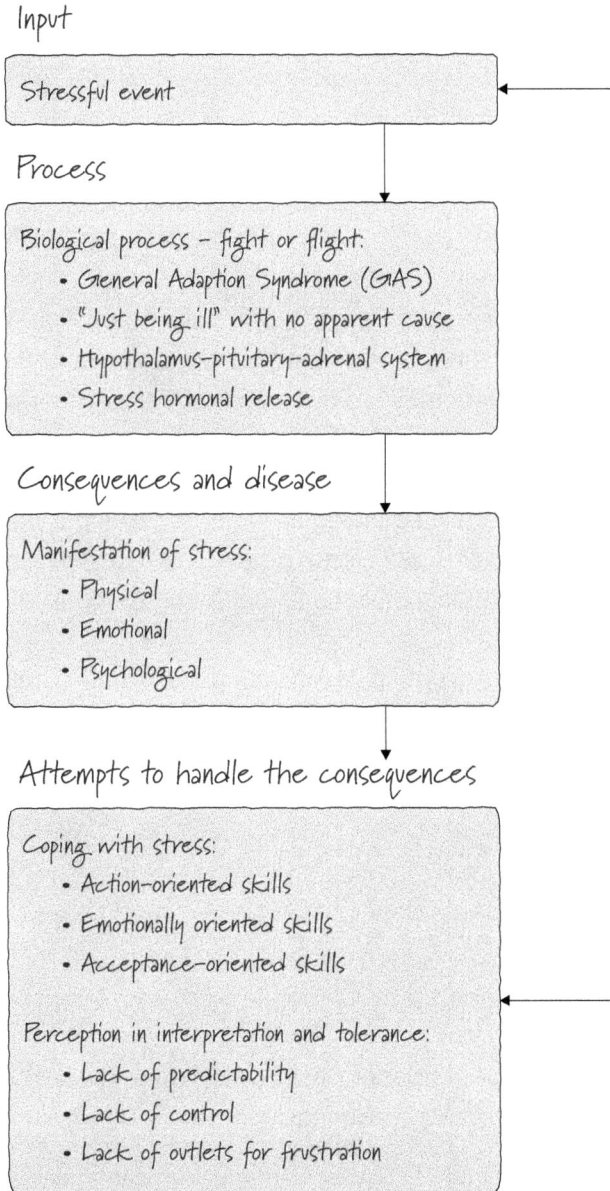

Input

> Stressful event

Process

> Biological process – fight or flight:
> - General Adaption Syndrome (GAS)
> - "Just being ill" with no apparent cause
> - Hypothalamus-pituitary-adrenal system
> - Stress hormonal release

Consequences and disease

> Manifestation of stress:
> - Physical
> - Emotional
> - Psychological

Attempts to handle the consequences

> Coping with stress:
> - Action-oriented skills
> - Emotionally oriented skills
> - Acceptance-oriented skills
>
> Perception in interpretation and tolerance:
> - Lack of predictability
> - Lack of control
> - Lack of outlets for frustration

The process of "being stressed" in the above classical systematic approach is explained as follows:

INPUT

- Unavoidable stressors are everywhere, especially in our cities with traffic jams, pollution and excessive noise. We are also exposed to daily changes in our home and work environments. These stressors are not only unpredictable; they can be long-term.
- We have high expectations of ourselves and others. We continuously measure others against our own set of standards. But as they are our own standards, others are unlikely to meet them. This causes us stress and frustration.
- We feel we are not in control of our own lives, at work or home. We feel someone else makes the decisions on our behalf and we must fall in line. We blame others and feel victimized in the process, which allows us to justify our behavior and state of mind.
- We fail to take responsibility for our actions as we believe they are "a result of forces beyond our control". We become caught in a stress trap.

PROCESS

- The physiological process now kicks in. Firstly, we have an "alarm reaction", in which the body prepares itself for "fight or flight": a rapid heart rate, increased alertness, etc. We are not able to sustain this process for long.
- A second stage of adaptation ensues, where we attempt to build resistance to the stressor.

- Finally, the body enters a stage of exhaustion. Our body releases stress hormones, which, over a prolonged period, cause us physical harm.

CONSEQUENCES AND DISEASE

If the stressors and our perception of them persist, we experience physical, mental and emotional consequences:

- We feel ill, but we do not know what is wrong with us. We remain tired, irritable and feel helpless. We experience physical symptoms, such as headaches, ulcers and hypertension.
- On an emotional level, we experience anger, mood swings and depression.
- On a psychological level, we experience nightmares, compulsive behaviors and addictions. The smallest issue sends us off the handle and we have difficulty controlling emotional outbursts. This makes us feel guilty.
- We no longer feel in control of our environment or ourselves. We try to find reasons and factors to blame.
- We seek medical help to treat the consequences and symptoms.
- Our perception of stress and what it does to us is reinforced.

ATTEMPTS TO HANDLE THE CONSEQUENCES

- We seek alternative methods to relieve stress. There are countless seminars and books on the subject. Many of them give the same message: learn to relax, practice yoga and get yourself a coach. These methods have value but are often difficult to maintain.

- We are told to change our environment, e.g. change jobs or relationships.
- We are led to believe we cannot change certain things and must simply accept them.
- We fall back into old habits, finding it difficult to break free from conditioned responses.

The above model demonstrates how our inability to effectively handle stress can cause us *more* stress. One becomes trapped in a vicious cycle of emotional and physical illness.

THE MIND-BODY CONNECTION

Humans can withstand extraordinary environmental stressors – to a point. If pushed too far, our stress response turns on our bodies and creates mental and physical breakdowns. When exhausted, the body is unable to return to its normal metabolism to rebuild its reserve of tissue and energy. This, in turn, has a profound impact on our state of mind.

According to Chopra, the mind-body connection includes invisible elements, such as interpretation, beliefs and attitude. These have implications in the workplace – for yourself and your ability to lead, and the well-being and productivity of your team.

WORKPLACE WELLNESS

Most companies conduct an annual "health check" survey to determine their employees' wellness at work. Employees are asked to complete a series of questions based on their perceptions of the company and their work environment.

Typically, the questions are grouped in the following categories:

- The ability of supervision generally.
- The performance and reward systems of the company.
- Diversity and the perceived or actual company tolerance of issues, such as harassment.
- Whether employees experience workplace stress.

All the questions are asked from a perception-based point of view. For most companies, questions about employees' experience of workplace stress consistently receive unfavorable answers. Typical questions in this regard center around:

- Whether employees feel equipped to do their jobs.
- Whether they can complete their work within the prescribed working hours.
- Whether they feel excessive workplace stress.

Year after year, company surveys reveal that employees feel stressed. Many employees believe their stress increases each year. This affects overall employee satisfaction, as they feel they have no control over their lives at work. The threat of corporate restructuring, mergers and acquisitions are potential hazards and employees long to be in charge of their destiny.

CHANGING THE WAY WE COPE WITH STRESS

Is it possible to cope with stress in a completely different way? Is it possible to transform stress from a tough or negative experience to something positive – something that could be accessed and used as an opportunity?

It is possible, provided you:

- Change your interpretation of the stressor or event.
- Make a mind-body-disease connection.
- Change your perception of stress by looking inward instead of outward.

"I believe if work is keeping you awake at night, you're either not doing your job during the day, or doing the wrong job. I would hate to think that I've got people in my organization who can't sleep because of work."

David Greer, OBE, FIMechE CEO, Serco Middle East, Africa and India, and Executive Committee Member of Serco Group

THE ALCHEMY OF STRESS

Alchemy is the medieval forerunner of chemistry. It is concerned with the transmutation of matter. In particular, alchemists have tried to convert base metals into gold or to find a universal elixir. It is regarded as a seemingly magical process of transformation or creation.

While there is nothing magical about experiencing stress, there certainly are opportunities to transform our mindset, attitude and outlook towards stress.

Wuzhen, a small town in the northern Zhejiang Province of China, is known as the Venice of the East and produces a refreshing, heady rice wine. The town was built along ancient canals and is known for its winemaking feats. Wuzhen had more than 20 wineries during the Ming Dynasty (1368-1644), but only one has survived to this day.[12]

San Bai Rice Wine is popular for its rich flavour and refreshing fragrance. San Bai, which means "three whites", refers to the three ingredients used for winemaking: rice, water and jiuqu (a culture of yeast and bacteria). The rice is soaked, cooked and cooled. When the yeast is added, the fermentation process starts. It takes up to three years for rice wine to mature.

The transformation of rice into wine is an art. This ancient and manual operation ensures no one pot of rice wine is ever

---

12 Sun Yuanqing, "Secrets of a dynasty-era winery," *China Daily*, February 20, 2015. http://europe.chinadaily.com.cn/epaper/2015-02/20/content_19620288.htm

the same. An elderly winemaker, Shen Jinchao, says, "Why this barrel tastes different from that one and why this gets ripe sooner than that one, these questions are always in my head."[13]

Stress can be compared to this ancient art of rice wine making. Just as yeast and bacteria are added to a pot of rice and water and left to ferment, our lives are filled with stressors, leaving us to ferment and fizzle. Do we allow these factors to cause us to pop our cork or do we use them to our advantage, creating a beautiful, mature wine in the process?

According to the ancient San Bai Rice Wine-making process, the ingredients and method are always the same. How the wine matures and what it ultimately tastes like depends on the skill of the wine-maker and his ability to use the transformational process to create a sought-after wine. Similarly, stress provides us with a powerful catalyst.

How do we choose to make our wine?

13 Sun Yuanqing, "Secrets of a dynasty-era winery," *China Daily*, February 20, 2015. http://europe.chinadaily.com.cn/epaper/2015-02/20/content_19620288.htm

TRANSFORMING STRESS

We must consider the possibility that our beliefs and attitudes about stress are what cause us so much tension, rather than the external stressors themselves. We must move from being a victim towards the proactive process of understanding, investigating and questioning our responses.

This requires a whole new way of thinking. We need to access the alchemy or transformational properties of stress. There are five key principles that will help you transform stress from a negative into a positive:

1. **Understand change.** How we cope and our ability to embrace change.
2. **Understand the power of your thoughts.** What we think is what we become.
3. **Practice meditation.** Develop and train the mind.
4. **Be mindful.** Be present and non-judgmental
5. **Be compassionate.** A key building block for mindful leadership and happiness.

Transforming stress through these principles is required on two levels:

1. **Outward.** Our behaviors and responses to stressors need to change. Do we fight, take flight or freeze? Or do we respond in a productive and positive way? This is the external or conscious change.
2. **Inward.** This relates to transforming our attitudes and belief systems. This is where permanent change takes place in our approach to stress and life.

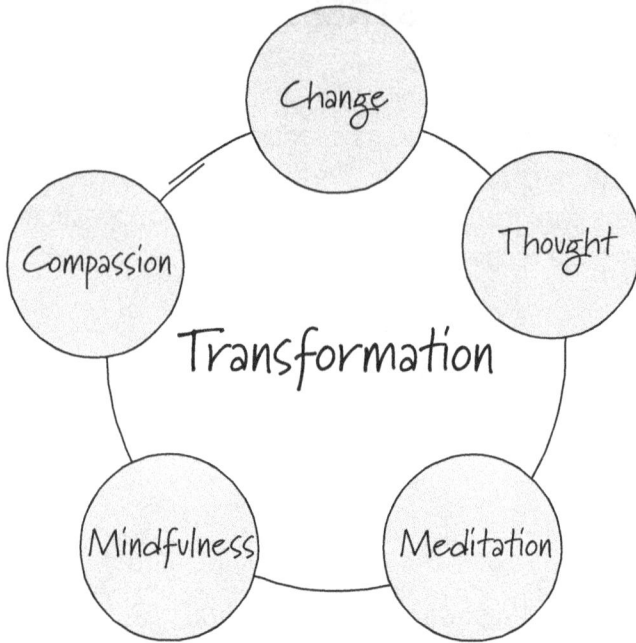

CHANGE AND ITS EFFECT

Change is a major source of stress. It challenges us to release the past, the comfortable ways of doing things, and to accept new opportunities for growth. There is an illusion that we manage change by controlling the world around us. Change, however, is most effectively managed from within. In the words of Mahatma Gandhi, "You must be the change you wish to see in the world."

To master change, one must look at the world through a new lens. As Scottish inventor Alexander Graham Bell wrote, "When one door closes another door opens, but we so often look so long and so regretfully upon the closed door, that we do not see the ones which open for us."

CHANGE IS CONSTANT

Author John Kehoe educates people about the fundamental law of constant change. This law states that everything in our lives is constantly in the process of becoming something else.

Kehoe explains: "Nothing stays exactly as it is. Nothing. Movement and change constitute the reality of our being. Our finances, our friendships, our career possibilities, our life opportunities, our health, our children, our parents, our daily activities, our insights, all are forever changing and becoming something else. To many, this is a frightening and daunting phenomenon, as most of us crave stability, but stability is an illusion, and you and your circumstances will change whether you like it or not, whether you want them to or not, because they cannot and will not remain the same. It is the law and nature of who we are as human beings having this extraordinary experience of living a life."[14]

You must understand and embrace change to have a happy and successful life. To change, you must recognize what needs changing. This involves turning inwards to reflect.

A poem by US author Portia Nelson illustrates this beautifully:

I walk down the street.
There is a deep hole in the sidewalk.
I fall in.
I am lost … I am helpless.
It isn't my fault …
It takes forever to find a way out.

---

14 John Kehoe, "The Law of Constant Change," John Kehoe: Mind Power. https://www.learnmindpower.com/article/law-constant-change/

I walk down the same street.
There is a deep hole in the sidewalk.
I pretend I don't see it.
I fall in again.
I can't believe I am in the same place.
But it isn't my fault
It still takes a long time to get out.

I walk down the same street.
There is a deep hole in the sidewalk.
I see it is there.
I still fall in ... it's a habit ... but,
My eyes are open.
I know where I am.
It is my fault.
I get out immediately.

I walk down the same street.
There is a deep hole in the sidewalk.
I walk around it.

I walk down another street.[15]

THE POWER OF OUR THOUGHT PATTERNS

Kehoe says if you want to make changes in your life, you must change the way you use your mind. This means looking at the way you think. A person cannot think negative and positive thoughts at the same time; one or the other dominates.[16]

---

15 Portia Nelson, *There's a Hole in My Sidewalk: The Romance of Self-Discovery*, Atria Books/ Beyond Words, 1988.

16 John Kehoe, "Mind Power Basics," John Kehoe: Mind Power. https://www.learnmindpower. com/using-mind-power/basics/

The mind is a creature of habit, so make positive emotions and thoughts the dominating influence. Train your conscious mind to think thoughts of success, happiness, health and prosperity. Weed out thoughts of fear and worry. Keep the conscious mind busy with the expectation of the best, and ensure your thoughts are based on what you want to happen in your life.

The conscious and unconscious minds work together to create our reality. Kehoe explains this with the following analogy:

"Your unconscious mind is like fertile soil which accepts any seed you plant within it. Your habitual thoughts and beliefs are the seeds which are being constantly sown within, and they produce in your life what is planted just as surely as corn kernels produce corn. You will reap what you sow. This is a law. Remember, the conscious mind is the gardener. It is our responsibility to be aware of and choose wisely what reaches the inner garden. But unfortunately for most of us, our role as gardener has never been explained to us. And in misunderstanding our role, we have allowed seeds of all types, both good and bad, to enter our inner garden."[17]

The unconscious mind does not discriminate between the positive and the negative. It will manifest failure, ill health and misfortune if they are the seeds we have planted.

The question then is: Can we change the unconscious mind? And if so, how?

Once we understand that our unconscious brings us what we desire, we must focus on the thoughts and images of what we want. Our mind will start to change and soon the unconscious

---

17 John Kehoe, *Mind Power into the 21st Century*, Zoetic, 2006.

will "bring to us" what we focus on. By changing our thinking and paying more attention to the present, we create a happier life.

THE CASE FOR MEDITATION

Meditation is a way of life. It is not a mystical process that will change who you are. Mediation is about becoming *more* of who you are. It helps you understand your life has direction and is unfolding. It enables you to slow down and deal with the fast pace of life. It costs nothing more than your time and is readily available anywhere, at any time.

Through the process of meditation and relaxation, the conscious mind empties itself of surface tension. Physical tension dissipates and the nervous system is temporarily cleansed. This is why meditation is so relaxing.

As we dive deeper within ourselves with regular meditation, we access higher, subtler energies within the mind. These energies infuse themselves within the unconscious mind where our patterns, biases and insecurities are stored.

Meditation is more than a means to calm the conscious mind and physical body. It is an ongoing process that enables us to find resolution and peace in many areas of our lives. With meditation, stress levels drop, you learn to relax and change is accelerated by a willingness to let go of blockages to success.

BENEFITS OF MEDITATION

Scientific studies show that meditation has the following powerful effects:

- Reduces stress.
- Lowers blood pressure and helps treat heart disease.
- Boosts immunity.
- Slows ageing.
- Reduces health costs.
- Helps manage chronic pain.
- Reduces mortality.
- Helps people suffering from chronic inflammatory conditions.
- Lessens the likelihood of recurring depression.
- Helps manage and prevent anxiety.
- Reduces feelings of loneliness.
- Promotes good sleep.
- Enhances mental clarity and emotional resilience.
- Increases self-compassion.
- Helps break through habits.
- Makes music sound better.
- Improves our working memory and academic performance.
- Rewires the brain for happiness.

BENEFITS FOR COMPANY EXECUTIVES

The popularity of meditation is growing amongst CEOs and senior executives. In fact, meditation appears to benefit leaders more than recreation or relaxation.

PART 2: LEADING SELF (SELF-MANAGEMENT)

Research on mindfulness also suggests meditation sharpens skills, such as attention, memory and emotional intelligence.[18]

The regular practice of meditation benefits leaders in the following ways:

- **It builds resilience.** Multiple research studies have shown that meditation has the potential to decrease anxiety, in turn boosting resilience and performance under stress.
- **It boosts emotional intelligence.** Brain-imaging research suggests that meditation can help regulate emotions.
- **It enhances creativity.** Research on creativity suggests we experience our greatest insights and breakthroughs – our "eureka" moments – when we are in a relaxed state of mind. This is likely because meditation encourages divergent thinking (i.e. coming up with the greatest number of possible solutions to a problem), a key component of creativity.
- **It improves relationships.** Stress narrows your perspective. It also reduces empathy, which negatively impacts performance. Meditation, however, can boost your mood and increase your sense of connection to others. It can even make you a kinder and more compassionate person.
- **It helps you focus.** Research shows our minds tend to wander about 50% of the time.[19] Add in work interruptions, text messages, instant messaging, phone calls and emails, and it's no surprise that leaders and employees have difficulty staying focused. Meditation training can help strengthen our ability to stay focused and even boost memory.

18 Emma Schoostra, Dirk Deichmann and Evgenia Dolgova, "Can 10 Minutes of Meditation Make You More Creative?", *Harvard Business Review*, August 29, 2017. https://hbr.org/2017/08/can-10-minutes-of-meditation-make-you-more-creative

19 Steve Bradt, "Wandering mind not a happy mind," *The Harvard Gazette*, November 11, 2010. https://news.harvard.edu/gazette/story/2010/11/wandering-mind-not-a-happy-mind/

MINDFULNESS

Being mindful is not about being lazy, escaping work by sitting cross-legged and meditating for hours on end. It is also not a quick fix for all work-related problems. It's about reducing and eliminating distractions. It's about enhancing personal focus and increasing awareness.

Mindfulness is highly applicable and relevant to our modern lives. Dr Jon Kabat-Zinn, a professor of medicine emeritus at the University of Massachusetts Medical School, says the most widely accepted definition of mindfulness is: "Paying attention to the present moment deliberately and non-judgmentally."

This definition is comprised of three parts:

1. **Paying attention to the present moment.** You may think you are present and paying attention all the time. How else do you read, drive a car or send an email? The truth is, we usually do these things without being fully present. We have learned to cope with distractions. Often, our thoughts are elsewhere – we are consumed with worries from yesterday and concerns about tomorrow. Being actively involved does not necessarily mean one is totally present.
2. **Deliberate action.** Being mindful is a deliberate action. We must be intentional with our approach to cultivating mindfulness.
3. **Without judgment.** Being non-judgmental is difficult. In this case, "judgment" doesn't mean a moral judgment; rather, it refers to an observation, such as "the coffee is hot," or perhaps someone says something that makes you think of something else. Disengaging from our constant mental commentary is probably the most challenging aspect of being mindful.

MINDFUL NEGOTIATIONS

I have always believed the "process is often more important than the end result". This is especially true in industrial relations. Negotiations between employer and employee are most successful when both parties feel valued and equally heard.

Traditional negotiations rely on the drafting of a carefully planned strategy prior to the start of negotiations. An opening, process steps, fallback positions and a final position are prepared. This works well in a structured environment, but it does have several downsides. The problem with such a structured plan is that negotiators may not get to "hear" one another. They are so preoccupied with the outcome that they fail to hear or understand what is being voiced.

The key to effective negotiations is to be mindful. Listen to what the other party has to say. Try to understand their point of view, place yourself in their shoes and practice empathy.

- **Listen attentively.** Be present when listening. It is easy to start formulating your side of the argument before you have even heard the other party out. Try to understand their point of view and ask questions to prevent misconceptions.
- **Be non-judgmental.** This is difficult but can be done if you deliberately try. Non-judgment is important when trying to understand someone else's point of view.
- **Empathy.** Place yourself in the other party's shoes. What would you do if faced with this decision or situation?
- **Explain.** It is far easier to reject a decision when one does not understand the reasoning behind it. Present your argument with substantiating facts and reasoning. It is easier to get

someone to accept a decision if they have all the information. They may not like it but will be more prepared to accept the outcome and move forward.

MINDFULNESS IMPROVES ORGANIZATIONS AND EMPLOYEES

Technological advancement demands round-the-clock responsiveness. It can simultaneously work in our favor and create havoc in our thought processes and ability to focus.

Our mobile phone constantly demands our attention. We continually scroll through messages, emails, news and social media. Often, we do this while we are in a discussion or having a meeting! Multi-skilling and mindfulness do not go together.

Mindfulness works. It eases stress, reduces health-care costs and improves productivity. Organizations are increasingly discovering that mindfulness and mindfulness programs are a powerful resource. Mindfulness programs can be a catalyst for positive change, improving:

- Attendance rates
- Staff retention
- Performance and job satisfaction
- Teamwork
- Personal relationships
- Creativity and innovation
- Leadership
- Sense of meaning and purpose

In fact, following a seven-week course at General Mills, there was a 60% increase in the number of staff who reported taking time each day to optimize personal productivity. There was also a 50% rise in staff taking time to eliminate tasks with limited productivity value. In addition, executives reported an 80% improvement in their ability to make productive decisions, while 89% reported they felt they had become better listeners.[20]

Intel has offered mindfulness training to employees since 2012. Its "Slowing Down to Speed Up" mindfulness program has shown encouraging results. Many participants have reported a decrease in their experience of stress, an increase in happiness and well-being, an improved ability to form new ideas and insights, and greater mental clarity, creativity, focus, quality of relationships and level of engagement in meetings, projects and collaboration efforts.[21]

Google also offers more than a dozen mindfulness courses. Google's most popular mindfulness course, "Search Inside Yourself," has thousands of alumni. Google believes mindfulness programs teach emotional intelligence, which help employees have a better understanding of their colleagues' motivations. They also boost resilience to stress and improve mental focus. Participants of the "Search Inside Yourself" program reported being calmer, more patient and better able to listen. They also said the program helped them better handle stress and defuse emotions.

From a management perspective, mindfulness permits employees to think. "Mindfulness is the essence of engagement. Being fully

20 Kimberly Schaufenbel, "Why Google, Target, and General Mills Are Investing in Mindfulness," *Harvard Business Review*, December 28, 2015. https://hbr.org/2015/12/why-google-target-and-general-mills-are-investing-in-mindfulness

21 Ibid.

present — and allowing your team to be fully in the moment — will reap rewards on a personal and professional level."[22]

Furthermore, mindfulness puts people in charge of their minds, attention and thoughts. It helps generate a stronger immune system, lowers blood pressure and heart rate, reduces stress and improves sleep. This positively impacts workers and shortens the amount of time they need to complete a task, thereby increasing productivity. Customer service, general work safety and teamwork all benefit.

MINDFUL LEADERSHIP

Mindfulness has many benefits to leadership. It helps you operate in the moment, gaining the psychological space you need to get in touch with work, projects, colleagues and the self. It enables you to focus on what is important. And it enhances creativity, allowing you to make the smartest choices and helping you become a more compassionate leader.

---

22 Kimberly Schaufenbel, "Why Google, Target, and General Mills Are Investing in Mindfulness," *Harvard Business Review*, December 28, 2015. https://hbr.org/2015/12/why-google-target-and-general-mills-are-investing-in-mindfulness

BEAUTY IN SIMPLICITY

South African coastal towns are known for their beauty, and the village of Stanford is no exception. Nestled beneath the beautiful Klein River Mountains, Stanford is picture perfect.

One day, to capture the beauty of a field of wildflowers, I lay flat on my stomach, hoping to get a good shot of the flowers, sky and mountain. As I prepared my camera, I heard the unmistakable sound of a country bicycle headed my way. I waited, hidden in the flowers. As the cyclist appeared in my photo frame, I snapped him. It was the proverbial perfect shot! The mountains, clouds, flowers and cyclist with only his thoughts to accompany him made the image beautiful in its simplicity.

Apple co-founder Steve Jobs said, "That has been one of my mottos – focus on simplicity. Simple can be harder than complex. You have to work hard to get your thinking clear to make it simple. But it is worth it in the end because once you are there, you can move mountains."

We tend to look for complex, difficult solutions. A simple or easy answer is often overlooked due to the belief it is "too good to be true". Working in industrial relations, I have often found the process is more important than the result, and often, the answer has been a relatively simple one.

Simplicity is also evident in relationships. We think they are complex when, in fact, it is only our thinking that makes them so.

Keep issues simple. Don't allow the intellectual component to take precedence – allow space for the heart. True leadership requires understanding and the ability to accommodate hearts and minds in problem-solving.

How do we create simplicity in our lives? I believe it is all in our approach to people – how we interact, how we listen and how we respond.

We should:

- **Stop thinking all the time.** Be present more and think less. Incessant thinking, arguing and analysing creates noise, preventing us from listening and understanding what we need to.
- **Practice mindfulness.** Pay attention to what you do. Pay attention to what is around you and be in the moment.
- **Be deliberate.** Cultivating mindfulness is a deliberate action. It involves a conscious decision and an active awareness.
- **Suspend judgment.** Disengage from the constant mental commentary.

In the words of author and productivity expert Bill Jensen, "Simplicity is power. The power to do less of what does not matter and more of what does."

PART 2: LEADING SELF (SELF-MANAGEMENT)

In conclusion, mindfulness means being present, deliberately and without judgment. It cultivates gratitude for our experiences. If we pay attention to the present, we are more likely to be happy – we don't get caught up in what we do not have or what we wish we had. The following story illustrates this.

THE STORY OF THE FISHERMAN AND THE INVESTMENT BANKER

An American investment banker was at the pier of a small coastal village in the Caribbean when a small boat with one fisherman docked. Inside the small boat were several large yellowfin tuna.

The American complimented the fisherman on the quality of his fish and asked how long it took him to catch them. The fisherman replied, "Only a little while."

The American asked why he didn't stay out longer to catch more fish. The fisherman said he had enough to support his family's immediate needs.

The American then asked, "But what do you do with the rest of your time?"

The fisherman said, "I sleep late, fish a little, play with my children, take siestas with my wife, Maria, and stroll into the village each evening where I sip wine and play guitar with my friends. I have a full and busy life."

The American scoffed. "I have an MBA from Harvard and can help you," he said. "You should spend more time fishing and with the proceeds, buy a bigger boat. With the proceeds from the bigger boat, you could buy several boats, and eventually you would have a fleet of fishing boats.

"Instead of selling your catch to a middle-man," the American continued, "you could sell directly to the processor, eventually opening up your own cannery. You could control the product, processing and distribution.

"Of course, you would need to leave this small coastal fishing village and move to a large city, where you will run your expanding enterprise," the investment banker concluded.

The fisherman asked, "But how long will this all take?"

The American replied, "Oh, 15 years or so."

"But what then?" asked the fisherman.

The American laughed and said, "That's the best part. When the time is right, you would announce an initial public offering, sell your company stock to the public and become very rich. You would make millions!"

"Millions – then what?" asked the fisherman.

The American said, "Then you could retire. Move to a small coastal fishing village where you could sleep late, fish a little, play with your kids, take siestas with your wife, and stroll to the village in the evenings where you could sip wine and play guitar with your friends."

– *Original author unknown*

NUMBING THE PAIN

I experienced a particularly stressful and challenging time in my life some years ago as an expat in China. One day at the office, I was feeling desperate and stressed out. There was a lot of chatter in my head about the difficulty I was going through, and I saw no easy way out. Taking medication to "calm my nerves" was not something I would typically do, but I was desperate enough to visit a doctor for a prescription.

I explained my situation to him and asked for something to help me cope. To my surprise, the doctor started talking about his issues and the difficulties he had been going through for some years. He seemed utterly despondent, needing more help than me! We had a good talk as I helped him with some thought processes. We both felt a whole lot better afterwards. I realized then that there is always someone else worse off than ourselves – and that helping someone else is often the best way to get ourselves out of a stressful situation. Needless to say, I did not need any medication and felt so much better about my own life.

Life will always present us with challenges, some quite character building! I choose to believe that things happen for a reason and I avoid feeling like a victim, as it takes us nowhere. We are in charge of our lives and the way we conduct ourselves.

COMPASSION

"I believe compassion to be one of the few things we can practice that will bring immediate and long-term happiness to our lives. I'm not talking about the short-term gratification of pleasures like sex, drugs or gambling (though I'm not knocking them), but something that will bring true and lasting happiness. The kind that sticks."
– Dalai Lama

Why is compassion so important and how does this help us transform stress from a negative to a positive? Is there is a difference between compassion and empathy?

American physician and Buddhist monk Barry Kerzin provides a practical explanation. He says compassion, in its fuller form, is altruism. Compassion can be the wish, commitment and action to reduce suffering. Initially, there is a wish to relieve suffering. As we develop more confidence, our commitment grows, which leads to action. Wisdom helps us see a broader perspective, so our action is successful.

This is different from empathy. Empathy is simply feeling what the other person is feeling. There is no commitment or action to lessen their suffering.

COMPASSION IS AUTHENTIC LEADERSHIP

A key ingredient of transformational leadership is the ability to be compassionate. Compassion, therefore, is an integral element of authentic corporate social responsibility (CSR). The story of the baby safe reflects this well.

THE BABY SAFE

A company I worked for a few years ago was involved in a profoundly emotional yet incredibly rewarding CSR event. The company supported an after-care center in an impoverished area of Pretoria, South Africa. The center reached out to the needy and those affected and infected by HIV and AIDS, providing programs such as skills development, a Saturday kids' club, life skills, mathematics classes and youth discipleship.

At the time, the impoverished community was struggling to cope with unwanted newborn babies. These babies were being abandoned and even discarded amongst the garbage at the city's refuse dump. The after-care center took the initiative to install a "baby safe".

The baby safe was a comfortable, warm, large post-box-type structure. It was designed so desperate mothers could anonymously place their unwanted baby in a safe environment where the child would receive immediate care. A camera monitored the box on a 24/7 basis and was connected to an alarm. The center management was alerted when a baby was left in the box.

This facility gave the community an alternative to abandoning unwanted babies. Our team became deeply involved with the initiative and supported the center through funding and participating in related activities, such as awareness campaigns for young women and school children. Educational materials and posters were also actively distributed. In addition, the team gave motivational talks to high-school students, encouraging them to practice safe sex.

I shall never forget the emotions we felt when two weeks after the baby safe had been installed, the center received its first unwanted newborn baby. We named the baby Fortune. This was one of the greatest moments of my corporate career. This intervention proved to be a great success, and in its first year alone, more than 11 newborn babies were received by the center via the baby safe.

The Dalai Lama often speaks about compassion. He says, "Compassion is necessary for life. It is necessary for our survival. A newborn baby would not survive without the kindness, affection and compassion of the mother. Without food, warmth, protection and shelter, the newborn would perish."

I believe authentic corporate responsibility is sometimes the difference between life and death. It is a critical component in the success of our day-to-day business. We are as good as the people we employ and the communities from which they come. It makes good sense for us to embrace our social responsibilities and ensure the well-being of those around us.

ACHIEVING PERMANENT CHANGE THROUGH EFFECTIVE SELF-MANAGEMENT

As we have seen, we can change our beliefs and attitudes towards stress. We are even able to influence how our body responds to stress. Permanent change is achieved within the unconscious mind. Change cannot be achieved without understanding the reasons for change and the consequences of not changing. We need to go through a process of self-discovery to gain this understanding.

We are capable of stress-free living, but we do need to change! The desire to change stems from the feeling that we are no longer in control of our lives.

There are generally two reasons why people would want to change:

- We see and feel the need to change within ourselves.
- We are forced to change because of external factors seemingly beyond our control.

SELF-AWARENESS LEADS TO SELF-MANAGEMENT

Achieving personal transformation is within your reach. To change, you must be aware of who you are and what it is that needs changing.

People react differently to stressful situations. We all experience tension, anxiety and insecurity in various ways. Some break out in a cold sweat and respond negatively to the smallest of situations, while others remain cool and in control in the face of impending disaster or provocation. Why such different reactions?

Perception shapes our view of reality. Our perception influences our thoughts and feelings. The issue, then, is not so much that the stressor – e.g. the next deadline or difficult task – causes us to react negatively. Rather, the issue is the way we view the stressor. Our perception of what is happening affects our reaction. How much of our depression, anxiety, fear, distress and worry could be reduced if we could change the way we saw problems? When you realize you can change your reality by changing your thinking, you will feel an incredible sense of freedom!

THE PRINCIPLES OF INTERNAL TRANSFORMATION

1. CUT THE STRINGS THAT TIE YOU

Free yourself from limiting thoughts, beliefs and behaviors. Examine your unconscious mind and recognize the source of your thoughts and reactions. By taking a good look inside yourself, you can see what needs to change – then, your journey towards balance, peace and happiness will begin.

2. GIVE UNCONDITIONALLY

When we give, we open ourselves to receive. And when we give, we need to do so unconditionally. This means expecting nothing in return. Always give only what you would be prepared to accept yourself. When it comes to receiving, always be grateful. Only through gratitude do we open ourselves to a life of abundance.

3. FORGIVENESS

Forgive yourself for who you are. It is only through forgiving yourself for what you think you have done that you can forgive others. We are driven by guilt and fear. Forgiveness provides us with an opportunity for release.

4. THE SECRET TO HAPPINESS

The ultimate secret to happiness is simple: choose to be happy! Happiness does not depend on anything other than a simple choice to be so. One makes a conscious choice to be happy regardless. We choose happiness in advance, and it is a decision to be made every day. Happiness is a choice, a state of mind!

5. DO YOU REALLY KNOW THE TRUTH?

It is important to keep in mind that what you experience is your perception. Based on your fears and inadequacies, it is easy to form unfounded assumptions about people and events. These, if we are not careful, become the basis of our thoughts and actions.

In situations where you believe someone is not being fair to you or working against you, ask yourself, "Do I really know the truth – is this a fact?" Once you have answered the question, and invariably you do not really know the truth, ask yourself how it would feel if you had not had the thought in the first place. Invariably, the answer is freedom!

PART 2: LEADING SELF (SELF-MANAGEMENT)

6. YOU ARE IN CONTROL - YOU ARE NOT A VICTIM

To believe your life is at the whim of chance, luck and fate is to give your power away, to become a victim of circumstances. This approach makes it easy to blame others and external factors for what you have become and for where you find yourself.

Choosing to be in control of your life puts the power back in your hands. Irrespective of what goes on in your life, know that you will always have a choice – either to do something differently or, at the very least, think about a situation in a different way. You have the power.

7. ENOUGH IS ENOUGH

Our lives are spent accumulating. It is easy to feel dissatisfied with what you have. Enough of anything can never be measured. It has no end. To experience a sense of fulfilment, choose to be content with what you have. Make full use of what you have and let go of what you no longer need to simplify your life and live contentedly.

8. OTHERS ARE MY MIRROR

It is interesting to note that often, what we so ardently dislike in someone else is what we struggle to acknowledge or deal with inside ourselves! It is not easy to see yourself reflected in another.

GRAVITY ISSUES

The most spectacular supermoon since 1948 lit up the sky on November 14, 2016. It appeared 14% bigger and 30% brighter than usual. American space agency NASA described the event as "undeniably beautiful". It was a result of the moon being closer to Earth than it had been for 68 years. Nothing will match it until the moon makes a similar approach on November 25, 2034.

I have taken photographs of the moon for some years, but this was not an event I wanted to miss. Living in Dubai, I was assured of a virtually cloudless, clear evening with only a little haze over the horizon. The appearance of the moon did not disappoint. Early in the evening, the moon appeared low on the horizon, a giant orange orb emerging from the haze. Undeniably breathtaking.

Having previously lived on the coast in South Africa, I often thought about the moon and its effect on the Earth and tides. The key to understanding the tides is to know the relationship between the motion of our planet, the moon and sun, and the role gravity plays. While the Earth spins on its axis, ocean levels are kept at an equal level around the planet by the Earth's gravitational pull. However, the moon's gravitational pull is strong enough to disrupt this balance by accelerating the water towards the moon, causing the water to "bulge", which we experience as a high tide.

Gravity is generally not something we think about. We don't wake up in the morning and think, "I hate feeling this heavy.

I would much rather be weightless and float!" We simply accept that gravity exists and understand it is not something we can do anything about.

I refer to business issues we cannot control as "gravity issues". A simple example is the current economic climate. Author Stephen Covey talks about the circle of concern and the circle of influence. The circle of concern is what we worry about, but we have no control over it. The circle of influence includes things we do have some control and influence over. Covey suggests that to be effective in business, one must separate lower and higher priorities in terms of which issues you have more control over. It is useless spending time and energy on things beyond your control.

To be effective as a leader, place areas of concern into one of the following three categories:

- **Gravity issues.** We cannot do anything about these matters of concern, they simply exist. We encounter them, but we cannot change them. Current economic or political conditions are examples of gravity issues. They are beyond our immediate control.
- **Issues we can influence.** These are matters we do not control but over which we do have some influence. For instance, we do not control what our partners or employees think or do, but we can influence their behaviors by the way we treat and talk to them.
- **Issues we control.** What we think, say and do are in our control, and so are our emotions. We decide how we want to feel and how people experience us.

Understanding and accepting what we can control, what we can influence and what is beyond our control is key to understanding the extent of responsibility in our lives. It serves little purpose to worry about matters we have no control over. By focusing on the "gravity issues", we stay stuck on the things we cannot change instead of making a difference to the things we can change.

Rise out of the haze, and you will have a lot more clarity about what you can do.

PART 2: LEADING SELF (SELF-MANAGEMENT)

9. I WILL JUDGE NOTHING

We tend to judge others according to our own standards and value systems. But who is to say that what you believe is true for someone else? It is dangerous to presume one can sit in judgment of another. Do not be quick to judge; instead, be ready to forgive. Accept and respect people for who they are.

10. ONLY LIVE IN THE NOW

This instant is all there is. We may believe we live in a fearful world full of suffering, conflict, depression and illness. We may worry unnecessarily about what we can no longer change and fearfully anticipate the future. But this allows us little time to focus on the most important part of our journey – the present! It is only by doing your best in this instant that you can create a future to look forward to.

THE EMPEROR'S THREE QUESTIONS – LEO TOLSTOY

One day, it occurred to a certain emperor that if he only knew the answers to three questions, he would never stray in any matter.

- What is the best time to do each thing?
- Who are the most important people to work with?
- What is the most important thing to do at all times?

The emperor issued a decree throughout his kingdom announcing that whoever could answer the questions would receive a great reward. Many who read the decree made their way to the palace at once, each person with a different answer.

In reply to the first question, one person advised that the emperor create a thorough time schedule, consecrating every hour, day, month and year for specific tasks and then follow the schedule to the letter. Only then could he hope to do every task at the right time.

Another person replied that it was impossible to plan in advance and that the emperor should put all vain amusements aside and remain attentive to everything to know what to do at what time.

Someone else insisted that, by himself, the emperor could never hope to have all the foresight and competence necessary to decide when to do each and every task, and what he really needed was to set up a Council of the Wise and then to act according to their advice.

Someone else said that certain matters require immediate decision and could not wait for consultation, but if he wanted to know in advance what was going to happen, he should consult magicians and soothsayers.

The responses to the second question also lacked accord.

One person said that the emperor needed to place all his trust in administrators, another urged reliance on priests and monks, while others recommended physicians. Still others put their faith in warriors.

The third question drew a similar variety of answers. Some said science was the most important pursuit. Others insisted on religion. Others claimed the most important thing was military skill.

The emperor was not pleased with any of the answers, and no reward was given.

After several nights of reflection, the emperor resolved to visit a hermit who lived on a mountain and was said to be an enlightened man. The emperor wished to find the hermit to ask him the three questions, though he knew the hermit never left the mountains and was known to receive only the poor, refusing to have anything to do with persons of wealth or power. So the emperor disguised himself as a simple peasant and ordered his attendants to wait for him at the foot of the mountain while he climbed the slope alone to seek the hermit.

Reaching the holy man's dwelling place, the emperor found the hermit digging a garden in front of his hut. When the hermit saw the stranger, he nodded his head in greeting and continued to dig. The labor was obviously hard on him. He was an old man, and each time he thrust his spade into the ground to turn the earth, he heaved heavily.

The emperor approached him and said, "I have come here to ask your help with three questions: When is the best time to do each thing? Who are the most important people to work with? What is the most important thing to do at all times?"

The hermit listened attentively but only patted the emperor on the shoulder and continued digging. The emperor said, "You must be tired. Here, let me give you a hand with that." The hermit thanked him, handed the emperor the spade, and then sat down on the ground to rest.

After he had dug two rows, the emperor stopped and turned to the hermit and repeated his three questions. The hermit still did not answer, but instead stood and pointed to the spade and said, "Why don't you rest now? I can take over again." But the emperor continued to dig. One hour passed, then two. Finally, the sun began to set behind the mountain. The emperor put down the spade and said to the hermit, "I came here to ask if you could answer my three questions. But if you can't give me an answer, please let me know so that I can get on my way home."

The hermit lifted his head and asked the emperor, "Do you hear someone running over here?" The emperor turned his head. They both saw a man with a long white beard emerge from the woods. He ran wildly, pressing his hands against a bloody wound in his stomach. The man ran toward the emperor before falling unconscious to the ground, where he lay groaning. Opening the man's clothing, the emperor and hermit saw that the man had received a deep gash. The emperor cleaned the wound thoroughly and then used his own shirt to bandage it, but the blood completely soaked it within minutes. He rinsed the shirt out and bandaged the wound a second time and continued to do so until the flow of blood had stopped.

At last the wounded man regained consciousness and asked for a drink of water. The emperor ran down to the stream and brought back a jug of fresh water. Meanwhile, the sun had disappeared and the night air had begun to turn cold. The hermit gave the emperor a hand in carrying the man into the hut where they laid him down on the hermit's bed. The man closed his eyes and lay quietly. The emperor was worn out from a long day of climbing the mountain and digging the garden. Leaning against the doorway, he fell asleep. When the rose, the sun had already risen over the mountain.

For a moment he forgot where he was and what he had come here for. He looked over to the bed and saw the wounded man also looking around him in confusion. When he saw the emperor, he stared at him intently and then said in a faint whisper, "Please forgive me."

"But what have you done that I should forgive you?" the emperor asked.

"You do not know me, your majesty, but I know you. I was your sworn enemy, and I had vowed to take vengeance on you, for during the last war you killed my brother and seized my property. When I learned that you were coming alone to the mountain to meet the hermit, I resolved to surprise you on your way back and kill you. But after waiting a long time there was still no sign of you, and so I left my ambush in order to seek you out. But instead of finding you, I came across your attendants, who recognized me, giving me this wound. Luckily, I escaped and ran here. If I hadn't met you, I would surely be dead by now. I had intended to kill you, but instead you saved my life! I am ashamed and grateful beyond words. If I live, I vow to be your servant for the rest of my life, and I will bid my children and grandchildren to do the same. Please grant me your forgiveness."

The emperor was overjoyed to see that he was so easily reconciled with a former enemy. He not only forgave the man but promised to return all the man's property and to send his own physician and servants to wait on the man until he was completely healed. After ordering his attendants to take the man home, the emperor returned to see the hermit. Before returning to the palace, the emperor wanted to repeat his three questions one last time. He found the hermit sowing seeds in the earth they had dug the day before.

The hermit stood up and looked at the emperor. "But your questions have already been answered."

"How's that?" the emperor asked, puzzled.

"Yesterday, if you had not taken pity on my age and given me a hand with digging these beds, you would have been attacked by that man on your way home. Then you would have deeply regretted not staying with me. Therefore, the most important time was the time you were digging in the beds, the most important person was myself, and the most important pursuit was to help me.

"Later, when the wounded man ran up here, the most important time was the time you spent dressing his wound, for if you had not cared for him he would have died, and you would have lost the chance to be reconciled with him. Likewise, he was the most important person, and the most important pursuit was taking care of his wound.

"Remember that there is only one important time and that is now. The present moment is the only time over which we have dominion. The most important person is always the person you are with, who is right before you, for who knows if you will have dealings with any other person in the future? The most important pursuit is making the person standing at your side happy, for that alone is the pursuit of life."

FOLLOW-THROUGH: THE ROADMAP TO INSIGHT IN SELF-MANAGEMENT

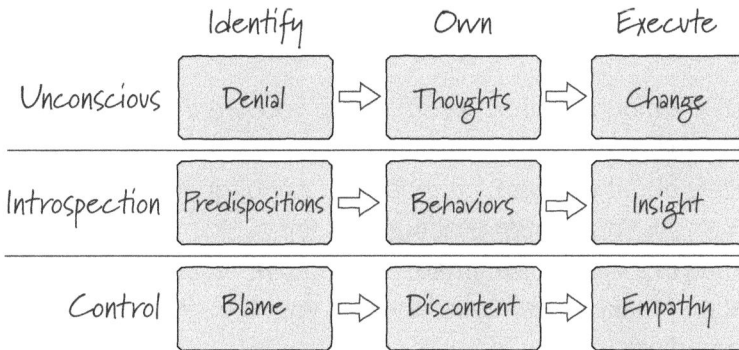

	Identify	Own	Execute
Unconscious	Denial ⇨	Thoughts ⇨	Change
Introspection	Predispositions ⇨	Behaviors ⇨	Insight
Control	Blame ⇨	Discontent ⇨	Empathy

Insight is about putting the strategic components of self-management to work. The roadmap to successful execution is through a process of **identification**, **ownership** and **delivery (execution)** of nine self-management components:

UNCONSCIOUS (MIND)

1. IDENTIFY YOUR DENIAL

Denial is a defense mechanism that allows you to block or refuse what you know is the truth or reality of a situation. You avoid rather than accept what is in existence. Denial manifests in three ways:

- **Rejection** of what is obvious. The refusal to acknowledge or accept what others know to be true of you.
- Rejection creates **internal conflict** as your unconscious mind knows the truth.

- This internal conflict creates **distress** through cognitive dissonance as you hold contradictory thoughts about the same situation.

2. OWN YOUR THOUGHTS

These are thoughts about yourself and your world. Your thoughts are a result of deep-seated beliefs in your unconscious mind – beliefs about who you are, what you stand for and the world around you. Your thoughts about yourself could be positive, resulting in a healthy self-image, or negative, resulting in a constant breaking down of oneself. In your thoughts, your reality is created:

- **Through belief.** We often think we are not good enough. We believe we deserve what we get, especially when the experience is negative. Believing in yourself, believing you are good enough, is not easy but it is certainly attainable.
- **Through trust.** Trust that it will work out. Trust you are on the right path. Most importantly, accept you must trust the process "of life". It will unfold in a way that is best for you, even if not immediately apparent.
- **Through hope.** Hope allows us to believe things can be different. Hope and trust go hand in hand: hope is based on a desire to change and transform, and trust is the knowledge it will happen.

3. EXECUTE CHANGE

This is where you have full control of creating change within yourself – what you think, say and do. However, self-awareness and an understanding of who you are is required. Change does not simply happen because you want things to be different or because you are being told a change is required. Change must first take place within your unconscious mind. We change our thought processes within our unconscious mind through:

- **Transformation.** Change through transformation is about developing a new version of yourself and your leadership
- **A shift in thinking.** Take a leap of faith. Transformational change is not supplemental; it is a mindset shift – a change in focus and the perception of your place in your world. It is your "ah-ha" moment of clarity.
- **Sustaining change.** Form new thought habits. This ensures the change is ongoing and transformational, not just for the moment.

EXECUTE CHANGE

Our lives never stay the same. Situations and circumstances are fluid and ever-changing. We may feel we are not in control of our lives. Sometimes, what worked for us yesterday suddenly stops being effective today and we are forced to change how we think and approach things.

Our daily thought patterns are based mostly on what has happened in the past and what we believe may happen in the future. Often, we spend time thinking about what could have been or what was. "Where are the good old days?" we ask. Typically, when we think about the "good old days", it is because we are either in a difficult situation or stressful time of change, which we feel is being forced upon us.

Change is not easy. It forces us to seek alternatives. Recognizing and finding new and alternative opportunities becomes easier if we follow the following process:

- **Acknowledge the past.** But do not remain there – certainly not in what you do, say or think. Whether the immediate past has been pleasant or not, move on and focus on what is, not what was.
- **Become more self-aware.** Think about what you are thinking. Think about what you see, feel and say. Become an observer more so than a participant. The immediate benefit is that you become much more objective about your situation.
- **Remember that new opportunities will arise.** Often, opportunities come disguised as something else. Be

prepared to recognize them for what they are. See the potential when they present themselves. Do not let your expectation become a limitation. By becoming more self-aware, it is easier to recognize an opportunity for what it is and for the potential it has.

Do you ever look back at the opportunities you missed? In hindsight, they seem so obvious, but at the time we did not recognize their potential. Doors are always opening. Stop staring at the closed door – it will not open again. Be open to change so when the next door opens, you are ready to step over the threshold into a new and exciting space in your life.

INTROSPECTION

4. IDENTIFY YOUR PREDISPOSITIONS

A predisposition is an inclination or tendency to behave in a certain way. Predispositions could be environmental or genetic (hereditary). Powerful influences outside your control also shape your predispositions during the impressionable stages of your life. Predispositions are shaped by the following:

- **Your environment.** Often, prejudices are formed during the early part of life. Think about prejudices regarding race and gender, for example. What prejudices were prevalent when you were growing up?
- **Your tendencies.** Your inclination towards a specific behavior. Tendencies are what you are most comfortable doing.
- **Your attitude towards life and others.** Your attitude is your settled way of thinking.

5. OWN YOUR BEHAVIORS

Behaviors are actions, the things we do with others and what we do to others. It's through your behaviors that people experience you. Your behaviors manifest in three ways:

- **Style.** How you present yourself.
- **Conduct.** How you behave and carry yourself with what you do and say.
- **Presence.** The impact you have on others and how you make them feel when you are in their space.

6. EXECUTE INSIGHT

Introspection provides insight. Insight means you can look within yourself and understand why you are who you are. You see yourself as others see you. You may also be able to understand why you think and behave the way you do. Insight enables one to change existing thoughts and behaviors. Support your insight through:

- **Regular reflection.** Reflection creates an awareness of who you are and what could be done differently.
- **Trusting your intuition.** Your intuition is based on your experiences and understanding of yourself. It is an intuitive feeling, a knowing.
- **Understanding your perception is just that – YOUR perception.** This is your reality. Remember, it is not everyone else's truth. Their perception is their world and it may differ from yours.

CONTROL

7. IDENTIFY BLAME

In its truest form, blame is to apportion responsibility to something or someone else. By saying "this is not my fault", we blame others for our failures. Identifying what is within our control, such as our thoughts and behaviors, is a crucial first step in understanding that blame is another form of being a victim. Blame consists of three components:

- **Guilt.** Blame is often driven by our guilt – guilt about something we have said or done and for which we are unable to forgive ourselves. An easy way out is to rationalize the issue and blame others or circumstances for our lack or inability.

- **Taking responsibility.** When you own your actions and behaviors, you effectively remove blame from the equation. Responsibility means accepting that your actions and behaviors are under your control. They cannot be blamed on something or someone else.
- **Being accountable.** No one is perfect. Being accountable for our actions – owning up to them and assuming responsibility for them in a transparent manner – also removes blame.

8. OWN YOUR DISCONTENT

It's common to experience a general lack of contentment with our circumstances, work and relationships. Often, we cannot put our finger on our discontent; we just know something is amiss. Discontent is prevalent under the following circumstances and you should identify each element as it relates to you:

- **Unhappiness.** We continually search for happiness. Often, we look at external factors to make us happy. We believe something or someone else could hold the magic key.
- There is **resentment** for what you do not have. You may also resent others for what they have achieved and what you have not.
- Closely related to resentment is **jealousy**. You may feel jealous of others' possessions and success, as you may think these things should be yours.

9. EXECUTE EMPATHY

Being empathetic means taking your focus away from blame, discontent and victimhood. Empathy is understanding the feelings of another by placing yourself in their proverbial shoes and looking at life from their vantage point. One can develop and nurture empathetic behaviors through:

- **Appreciation.** Appreciate others' qualities. It is easy to find fault in others, but it is far more rewarding to appreciate and recognize their value.
- **Gratitude.** Gratitude helps us be mindful of what we have. It teaches us awareness, empathy and compassion. This will help you understand another's position and guide you to assist when help is needed.
- **Understanding the issues of others.** When we make an effort to understand what others are going through, we realize our situation is not that bad.

THE IMPACT

To cope with our rapidly changing and challenging world, we are required to constantly adjust. But change, as we know, is one of the biggest causes of stress in our lives.

We discover that blaming others for our situation does not work. Importantly, the realization that we cannot change others, only ourselves, is required. We must adjust our thoughts, values, attitudes and behaviors. We must become inner-directed. We must utilize more of our consciousness to manage our lives more effectively.

PART 2: LEADING SELF (SELF-MANAGEMENT)

We are required to move from being stressed to having insight into our own thinking and behaviors through focus and clarity. Our goal, therefore, is to understand our unconscious mind better, what it takes to change and what we have control over. Through reflection, you can move away from being a victim to reclaiming your personal power and becoming a transformational leader. Ultimately, you need to embrace change and empathy.

The impact of successful self-management is as follows:

Below	Above
Resentful ✗	Compassionate ✓
Victim ✗	Forgiving ✓
Blame ✗	Mindful ✓
Denial ✗	Acceptance ✓
Stressed ✗	Freedom ✓

THERE ARE TWO REASONS
WHY PEOPLE CHANGE:
THEY EITHER SEE THE
LIGHT OR THEY FEEL
THE HEAT.

LEADING THE TEAM

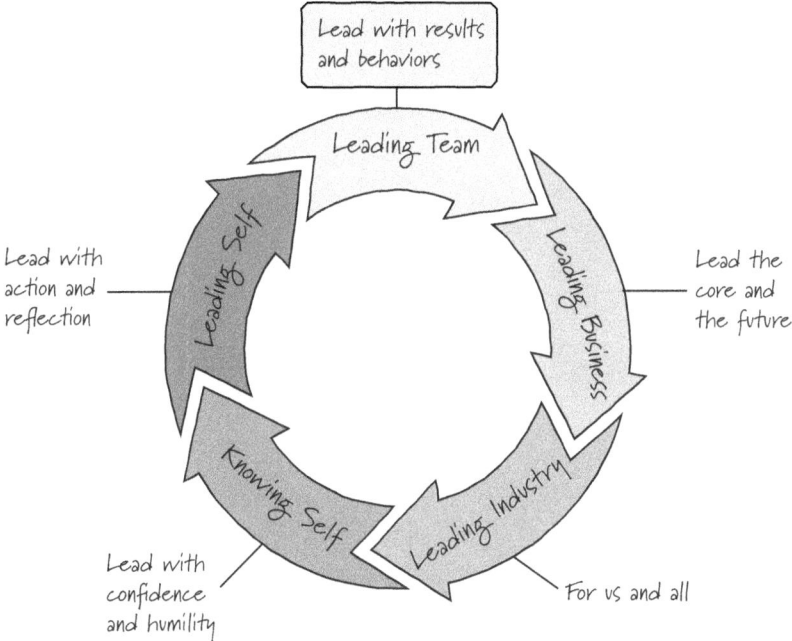

Lead with results
and behaviors

Leading Team

Leading Business

Leading Self

Lead with
action and
reflection

Lead the
core and
the future

Knowing Self

Leading Industry

Lead with
confidence
and humility

For us and all

PART 3

LEADING THE TEAM: LEAD WITH RESULTS AND BEHAVIORS

RELATIONSHIPS AND TEAM EFFECTIVENESS

Relationships and team effectiveness in business are key components of every successful enterprise. Relationships built in the absence of mutual respect and trust become toxic, resulting in a total lack of effective functioning. In business, for a workgroup or team to function effectively, there should be a sense of group cohesiveness and trust between team members.

For a relationship to be built on trust, team members must be reliable, open, honest and accepting of each other. Having each other's back is an essential element of forming a trust relationship. Looking out for each other, protecting each other and the effective offering of assistance and support means you have each other's back.

Nothing happens by itself. Purposeful planning and execution by the leader and the team are required every day. Ultimately, everyone in the team and the organization has a place and a role to play. There is no one member more important than another. Each has their responsibility. Each effective individual ensures the success of the entire team.

STRATEGIC PERSPECTIVE: LEADING TEAMS

RELATIONSHIP MODEL SUPPORTING TEAM EFFECTIVENESS

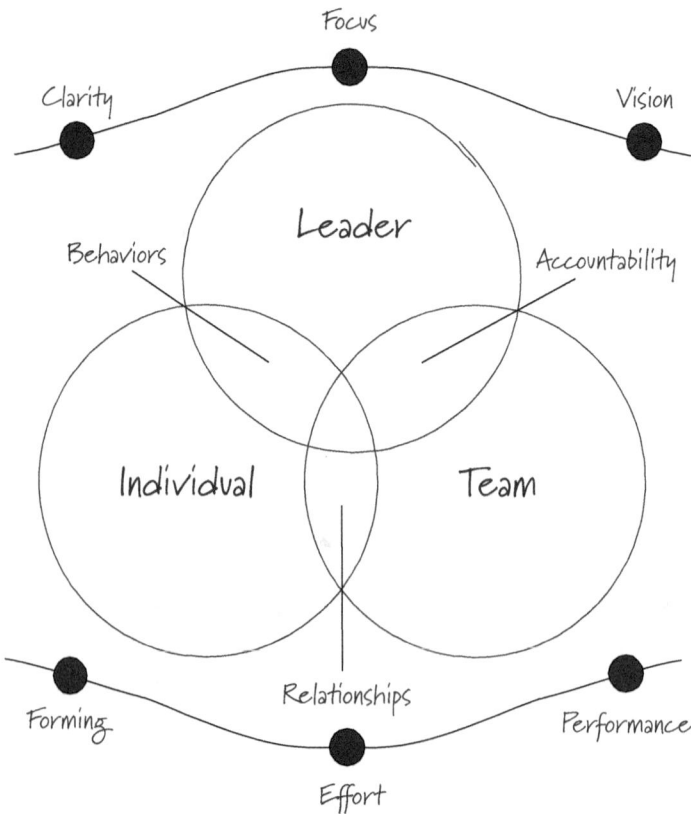

Focus

Clarity

Vision

Leader

Behaviors

Accountability

Individual

Team

Forming

Relationships

Performance

Effort

The three core components of a team are:

- Team leader
- Individual
- Team

The effectiveness of a team is the function of the leader's profile, individual behaviors and group dynamics. The level of maturity at which the team operates depends on how each component interacts. Types of behavior, relationships and levels of accountability are the outcomes of these interactions.

At the three intersections are:

- **Behaviors.** These relate to those of the individual, the team leader and the general behavior of the team.
- **Relationships.** These refer to the bonds – or lack thereof – between team members, members and their leader, and the relationship between one team and another.
- **Accountability.** The individual and group must be accountable for what the team produces.

WHAT DOES LEADING THE TEAM MEAN?

I distinctly remember being appointed supervisor at the beginning of my HR career. I was young and this new role was incredibly daunting and difficult. I quickly realized my success as a leader was directly linked to the success of my team. I could no longer do all the work myself and had to learn to delegate and trust.

This was my introduction to team dynamics. To be productive, I had to rely on others. I had to motivate them to do things the way

PART 3: LEADING THE TEAM

I wanted them done. I also had many expectations, which I soon realized were not going to be met.

It can be challenging to accept that the people you supervise will never do the work exactly the way you want them to or the way you would have done it. But I realized a critical thing – the more I provided guidance only (and less direction), and allowed for their creativity, the better the results. The lesson I learned early in my career was that we should trust people to do the best they can and not keep directing the what and how of their task. Of course, there will be mistakes, and at times great disappointment, but overall I came to appreciate the value of putting trust in people to do the best they can.

"When I came into this role, the most critical thing for me was to surround myself with the right people. Build my team, surround myself with the people I knew I could trust. They had a similar mindset to me and a similar passion for the business. That, for me, was the number-one priority.

"We planned where we wanted to take the business and we set ourselves some pretty ambitious goals, doubling the size of the business every five years. From there, it was a case of, well, then we have to train and develop our staff to get them up to speed so that we can achieve those numbers.

"Everything we've done has been a fantastic team effort by great people I've worked with. That, to me, is one of the most critical things because as a leader, you can't do it on your own. We have pressure to hit quarterly numbers, we have pressure to hit half-year and full-year numbers, but to hit those numbers, you've got to know where you're going with the business.

"The other day, we were planning the budget for next year and we were saying, 'Jeez, we have to hit 20 million on average per month profit before tax,' and one of my people said, 'How are we going do that?' I reminded him, 'You will remember, five years ago we were having the same discussion about hitting 10 million.' We have to be clear in our minds where we want to go with the business and put a plan in place and stick to that plan. You know you're going to have to tweak your plan as you go, because it's never going to be 100% right. But if you tweak it according to what's happening in the economy and technology, etc., and you get the buy-in of all your people, then you're already halfway there."

Gary Neubert
CEO, EIE Group
Johannesburg, South Africa

WHAT IS TEAM EFFECTIVENESS?

An effective team is one that reaches its objectives. It also helps the broader organization achieve results. However, a team's effectiveness is evident not only in the results it produces – it's also in the dynamics between members and leaders.

The Five Dysfunctions of a Team[1] presents the notion that teams are inherently dysfunctional. Therefore, deliberate steps must be taken to facilitate great teamwork. A knowledgeable team leader can do a great deal to make his or her team effective, and the book outlines practical tools to achieve this.

Great teamwork gives you and your organization a commanding competitive advantage. The problem is, it is not easy to accomplish, as organizations generally have a hard time avoiding the common dysfunctions of a team. The foundations for great teamwork are laid by building trust, engaging in constructive conflict, committing to decisions, holding peers accountable and focusing on common goals.

For a team to be effective:

* The team leader must continually evaluate the business environment and raise objectives that are relevant and impactful. This is not a once-a-year exercise. It is ongoing and must involve the rest of the team.
* The leader must recognize the team's strengths and weaknesses. Be aware of each member's level of competency, as well as their individual skillsets. A transformational leader

---

1 Patrick M. Lencioni, *The Five Dysfunctions of a Team: A Leadership Fable,* John Wiley & Sons Inc., 2002.

"My second comment is around inspirational leadership and teamwork with all the technology apparently doing the thinking, and people just collating. There was a very interesting article I read that said teamwork shouldn't be measured when things are working normally. Then all teams would be high-performance teams. Teams should be measured when in crisis.

"Consider the Thailand cave rescue (in 2018). When you don't have time to group, regroup, send emails and get opinions, you're working against the clock and you must save lives. There was not a lot of team building done before they rescued the 14-odd kids from the cave. Management needs to get to a point where they can assemble and motivate a team under such conditions. That is real leadership, and that is real teamwork."

Henda Smit
CEO, The Makings, Industrial Psychologist
Johannesburg, South Africa

will spend time developing individual members, building on their strengths and addressing their weaknesses.
- The team and leader must understand the environment the team operates in so it can anticipate external threats and opportunities.
- The team and leader should have a holistic view of the business. It is not good enough to understand only one area – an overall understanding is crucial. What are the drivers of the business? What opportunities are there to be found? What are the obvious threats?

- All members must be accountable – to the business, themselves and the team.
- Team leaders must also be teachers and coaches. They are responsible for the well-being of the team, which means life-coaching skills are necessary. As the team leader, how can you help and support members who are struggling?
- The right talent must be identified and selected. There should also be some diversity among team members.
- Team members must be able to interact with each other and the leader effectively. Team dynamics determine team success.
- The leader must manage the team's talent lifecycle effectively. This means knowing how to retain talent and when to bring new people on board.

WHAT IS A SUCCESSFUL TEAM LEADER?

The effectiveness of any team relies heavily on its leader. A successful team leader knows how to instil confidence in their team, build trust and help the organization grow through their team's productivity.

THE EIGHT QUALITIES OF A SUCCESSFUL TEAM LEADER

1. Establish a compelling direction and vision through setting the strategy.
2. Build a competent and robust structure.
3. Oversee a strong governance process of accountability.
4. Give team members constructive feedback and a balanced performance review process.
5. Effectively handle conflict.
6. Engender and own working together.

7. Oversee the talent lifecycle process.
8. Lead by teaching, coaching, mentoring and role-model behaviors.

Let's look at these eight qualities in greater detail.

1. ESTABLISH A COMPELLING DIRECTION AND VISION – DETERMINING THE STRATEGY

This is an essential first step for any team leader. Establishing a direction and vision helps the team set solid objectives, realistic targets and metrics, and adopt a viable strategy.

A strategic planning process encourages people engagement, fosters team members' commitment to their roles and delivers business results. The strategy itself inspires people to act. This means team members' roles and responsibilities must be clearly set out and understood.

A strategy is an executable plan that develops the following:

- A sense of common purpose.
- Ownership of day-to-day operations and business results.
- A culture of accountability and responsibility.
- Clarity on key priorities.
- A robust governance process.
- An effective, functioning leadership team.

PART 3: LEADING THE TEAM

"Creating, believing in and translating a clear vision is one of the great leader's attributes, along with trust, respect, motivation, openness and influence. Moreover, great leaders owe their teams the protection and support to eliminate obstacles and achieve their objectives.

"To support my holistic point of view of the main attributes of great leaders, I can add that:

- Leaders master effective listening skills.
- Leaders think strategically and communicate clearly (and here I can relate to my discussion on having a clear vision. A vision is the dream that will enable the team to see the tangible impacts of their dedication and hard work).
- Leaders celebrate success and create an environment of appreciation and recognition.
- Leaders consider resources utilization as an art.
- Leaders spread positivity and encourage collaboration.

"Finally, I must say that great leaders must set an example for the team on how and why to accomplish goals. I'm here referring to building and living by the culture that defines the way of doing things."

Hassan Chalak
Regional HR Manager, Posta Plus
Kuwait

To be effective, a team leader must have utmost clarity about the team's vision, strategy and direction. You must know what the team is required to do and ensure members have a thorough understanding of the processes involved – there can be no guesswork.

Effective communication is paramount to a productive strategy and successful team.

The process of creating a strategy is as follows:

- Define and set a direction.
- Define strategic intent.
- Determine high-level priorities.
- Determine an actionable outcome.
- Develop and implement a governance process to deliver outcomes and enhance team effectiveness.

It also requires the analysis and determination of the following:

- The business environment – both external and internal.
- Opportunities, traits and benchmarks in other industries.
- Your customers.
- Your products and services.
- Deliverables and metrics that measure top priorities.

Strategy requires constant review and fine-tuning. It is not a once-off process. While your strategic vision and intent may not change, sometimes it is necessary to adjust your direction. The tactical execution of a strategic plan means going back to your objectives, assessing what you are delivering, identifying gaps and adjusting accordingly.

"I like to tell my people, 'Look, I'm going to let you know now, there's not a single mistake you can make that I haven't made before, and far worse.' Setting that environment that says, 'Hey, if you want to look for the first person who's imperfect, it's me.' When leaders openly talk about their own mistakes, it helps people feel that humanity and creates that safe environment.

"What always influenced me was the Stockdale paradox. The guys in Vietnam who went crazy in the prisoner-of-war camps were the ones whose captains would tell them, 'Don't worry, I've heard we're getting help by Christmas.' Christmas came and went and they're still there. Then they were told we're getting out by Valentine's Day. Valentine's Day came and went and they were still there. And Admiral (Jim) Stockdale, he simply told the guys, 'We are getting out of here. I don't know when. I don't know how. But I do know we're going to do it.' It was that kind of confidence, without giving people some sort of airy-fairy thing to look forward to. He did instil in them the confidence that we're on this, we're going to get through this. How? We don't know yet and that's OK.

"It's important for leaders to say we don't have all the answers, but we are committed to getting through. We're going to hit rough times. When we do, we're going to figure it out. That's the kind of solid, steady leadership we need. I think Alan Mulally at Ford did it really well, because it was develop the plan, work the plan. That's it. Lather, rinse, repeat. Develop the plan, work it, and measure yourself to the plan."

Kris Kumfert
Chief Human Resources Officer, Clark Pacific, California, USA

2. BUILD A STRONG AND COMPETENT STRUCTURE

A team's structure must be based on its strategy. Team leaders usually design a structure around people, but for a team to be effective, the structure must first take into consideration the work that needs to be done.

There are three components to developing a strong and competent structure:

1. Have a clear understanding of your strategy.
2. Once the strategy is established, determine the specific roles and responsibilities of team members.
3. Understand the products, processes and services required to be delivered and sourced through the structure.

"I find the Johari concept fascinating in that when I'm going slow with people, I will strive to find out what makes people tick. The more I know about them, and the more I know what they know about me, the less of the 'what we don't know' about each other. When you get people comfortable and you sense that openness and bonding between people, you can achieve great things. You can be sympathetic to their fears, but equally you can reinforce those things they are really good at. And sometimes we don't do that. We tend to put teams together and I don't think we put enough time into selecting personalities for teams.

"How often have you seen teams fail because they put six passengers in a team? And equally, how many have failed when you put six drivers in a team? That goes nowhere. Getting that optimum mixture of people – a driver, a thinker, maybe a couple of passengers – is absolutely key to getting things done. And very often, we don't spend enough time doing that."

David Greer, OBE, FIMechE
CEO, Serco Middle East, Africa and India, and Executive
Committee Member of Serco Group

3. OVERSEE A STRONG GOVERNANCE PROCESS OF ACCOUNTABILITY

A strong governance process ensures the team delivers its objectives. A governance process highlights accountability, responsibility, metrics and specific targets. It is designed to execute the strategy. This means ensuring objectives are time bound and assigned to specific individuals.

An essential element of a strong governance process is a robust review process, where metrics and targets are reviewed on a regular basis.

"The way I see the leadership role, what will create success for any leader at this level would be your ability to think at different levels. This means, firstly, thinking at 50,000 feet at a strategic level. Secondly, it means being able to put it across at the operational level and, thirdly, to be able to complete the cycle on the execution level, at the five-feet level. To me, the number-one criterion for any successful leader is not just to get stuck at 'I can only think strategically' or 'I can think only execution'.

"I've seen a lot of leaders get stuck at their comfort leadership altitude of operational level or strategic thinking, not knowing how to execute their plan. To me, successful leadership lies between strategic thinking, good execution and looking forward."

Chhitiz Kumar
CEO, Philips Capital, Middle East and Turkey,
United Arab Emirates

4. GIVE TEAM MEMBERS CONSTRUCTIVE FEEDBACK AND A BALANCED PERFORMANCE REVIEW PROCESS

Transformational leaders give their team members quality feedback. This allows for healthy communication between the team's leader and its members, which is critical to the success of the team.

Feedback must be open and honest. A successful leader always gives credit where credit is due and raise areas of concern before they become greater problems. This type of communication should be ongoing and accessible to all members.

A balanced performance review process identifies shortfalls and opportunities for individual team members, which supports the growth of the team.

"One of the things we should endeavour to do as HR professionals is to put up the mirror to senior leaders from time to time. This can be something that is both positive and developmental, particularly if we avoid words that are critical.

"In my environment, there was a recent leadership meeting where I saw the behavior of a particular leader wasn't constructive, so I chose to intervene. It's always an option as an HR professional to intervene or not, then finding the opportune time to get that leader in the right place to talk them through what you've observed and to get their reflection of what happened. You can then provide an element of coaching and suggestion in terms of what they could do differently.

"That's one of the key things I internalize. Take an action, see what the outcome is and reflect on what went well, what didn't, what do I do differently next time. That's how I analyze myself and that's what I try to bring into the organization, both with the leadership team and the owner of the company. I think that's the first angle around developmental improvement in leaders – observing the truth in terms of what's happened.

"The other thing is when you're not getting progress, look for allies in the organization you trust and with whom you can reflect on your own observations and get some support. I look for support, particularly on people matters when I'm not being successful."

Stuart Daniels
Vice President, Human Resources, RMA Group
Bangkok, Thailand

PART 3: LEADING THE TEAM

GIVING AND RECEIVING FEEDBACK

As an amateur photographer, I realize my passion is
a personal representation of the world I see. However
noteworthy I feel it is, my photography is subjective and
possibly has many imperfections. Honest feedback from a
respected source gives me a balanced view of my work and
an opportunity to improve.

Dr John Izzo, an author and speaker in the business of
"conversations that make a difference", says it is important to
not only hear but effectively use feedback.

We must put our ego aside to process feedback. Our usual
reaction is to go on the defence and justify our actions. But
when we do this, we miss out on the value we could have
received by being open to constructive feedback.

The process for the effective giving and receiving of feedback
is as follows:

- **Purposefully look for opportunities to grow.** Constructive
  feedback is purposeful and mindful. It is well-considered
  and given in such a way that it is welcomed. Because
  it focuses more on the situation rather than the person, it
  is seen by the recipient as constructive, not as criticism.
  It is regarded as an opportunity for personal growth and
  development.
- **Receive feedback without defences.** If you can look at
  the situation objectively and without ego, you maximize
  the benefit of the feedback and learn.

172 | ANTON VAN DER WALT

- **Ask to tell me more.** The best technique to remove the ego is to respond with, "Thank you for the feedback, please tell me more." When we say this, we are less likely to become defensive.

As a leader, purposefully seeking feedback is as important as giving it. The ability to receive feedback without making excuses is a leadership quality that will help you grow and mature.

5. EFFECTIVELY HANDLE CONFLICT

Conflict presents potential stumbling blocks for any team. Different issues, priorities, objectives and levels of skill, experience and knowledge all provide fertile ground for conflict.

It is critical the team leader establishes a process for effective conflict resolution. If conflict is not handled constructively or positively, not only will the team suffer, the business will, too.

To handle conflict effectively, the team leader must encourage the following:

- **Trust.** When members know they can count on each other, it strengthens their bond. Morale is boosted, productivity increases and the team is more likely to deliver its objectives.
- **Robust debate.** Debate ensures issues are nipped in the bud early. It is far easier to discuss issues before they escalate into full-scale negative conflict.

- **Openness.** Team members need to feel safe to raise their concerns. When people are encouraged to be open and frank with what troubles them, it nurtures trust and team loyalty.

"I think leadership requires you to deal with more conflict. I like what Les Brown and T.D. Jakes teach you. They say the only thing that management pays you for is actually dealing with more conflict. If you can deal with more conflict, great, you get promoted and go up the corporate ladder.

"The second element of what you get remunerated for is your ability to execute. You invariably are going to be dealing with work on a much larger scale. I think it's not just the delegation of tasks; it's also about the execution of tasks. I found that leaders sometimes struggle between delegation and execution. You need to be at a point where you can execute consistently and delegate consistently.

"The third one I think that leaders need to know is when to step back and when to step forward. In the Zulu culture, they say sometimes taking two steps back is about gathering your strength. And taking a step forward is about demonstrating your strength."

Anthony Govender
CEO, ASI Financial Services
South Africa

6. ENGENDER AND OWN WORKING TOGETHER

The ability of the leader and team members to work together and for the good of the company is fundamental to the team's success. If people are unable to work together constructively, the team will never function properly.

Everyone in the team must cooperate and use their skills to support each other through challenging times. It's important they ask each other: What can I do to help? How can I help you resolve this? Are you in trouble?

The team leader should encourage collaboration between members. Clarify possible areas of concern and focus on the roles each member can play in contributing to the overall success of the team. It is all about connecting and creating formal and informal networks and structures that promote effective teamwork and communication.

7. OVERSEE THE TALENT LIFECYCLE PROCESS

The talent lifecycle process is a crucial element in the overall success of the team. It is critical the team leader sources the right talent, develops the talent correctly and ensures long-term retention. It is destabilizing for a team to have talent coming and going. Talent should be committed and engaged.

PART 3: LEADING THE TEAM

"I was at the ADT conference recently, and Marcus Buckingham was a keynote speaker. He discussed the importance of being able to capitalise on people's strengths rather than just focusing on their weaknesses. He gave an example of Lionel Messi, often considered the best football player in the world.

"At the age of 13, Messi relocated to Spain to join Barcelona. He had a very strong left foot and they tried to develop him as a more balanced player. They realised that he had an amazing left foot and strengthened this skill to the point where he is now regarded by many as one of the greatest players of all time.

"This story translates well to business. Quite often, we try to make our employees good at everything or we try to fit a square peg in a round hole and then wonder why they're not successful. The art of a good leader is being able to understand what is important for the team to deliver and then leveraging the strengths of the team to deliver the collective objective. If there are obvious weaknesses, you will need to support these but you should also celebrate and leverage the strengths of your employees. It not only benefits the organization but motivates employees, leading to better results for all."

Gayle Anthony
General Manager: Head of Global Learning and Development,
Nissan Motor Company
Nashville, United States

THE TALENT LIFECYCLE PROCESS

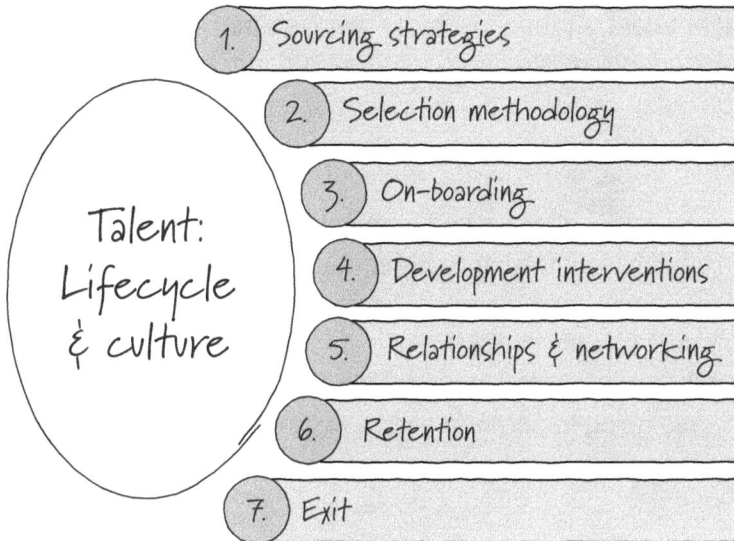

Talent: Lifecycle & culture

1. Sourcing strategies
2. Selection methodology
3. On-boarding
4. Development interventions
5. Relationships & networking
6. Retention
7. Exit

1. SOURCING STRATEGIES

These are what will help you find talent and determine their availability.

A CASE STUDY IN SOURCING

A few years ago, I was involved in setting up a new business unit in the Middle East and Africa region. As head of human resources, it was my job to source talent across all functions. It was a tall order, as it involved finding highly qualified professional people in finance, sales, marketing, product development, human resources, etc.

The company had budgeted a significant amount of money to spend with agencies and so-called head-hunters to find the right talent. At the time, most talent sourcing was done through agencies. We opted for a revolutionary approach. We looked at social media as a form of recruitment – in particular, LinkedIn.

Two years later, the team had recruited the entire regional office business unit using this approach. Between 200 and 300 people were recruited. Not a cent was spent on recruitment agency costs. We understood the market, we knew where we wanted to source, we understood where the talent was going to come from and we understood the talent itself.

2. SELECTION METHODOLOGY

Bias is not usually pre-meditated, but it is a potential stumbling block. It is human nature to recruit a person similar to oneself. That's why selection methodologies must be unbiased and create equal opportunities for diversity and gender equality. Selection methodology is evolving along with changes in technology. This means recruiters must not only scroll through databases for resumes, they must engage in audio interviews, face-to-face Skype interviews and connect via other social media hubs, such as WhatsApp and LinkedIn. Cognitive technology, machine learning and artificial intelligence will also come to play an integral role in the future of unbiased selection processes.

3. ONBOARDING

It is easy to get a new employee to sign documents, direct them to their desk, then leave them to their own devices. But how does this make them feel? Most successful companies realize the importance of making the new employee feel valued. A good onboarding program is an excellent way to start the process. This means investing time and effort into new recruits, even giving them a good two or three days in an induction process. Something as simple as showing a new team member to their workspace, which has been well prepared for their arrival, makes them feel valued and appreciated before they have even started their work.

It is also important the team's leaders introduce themselves to new members. Talk about the company culture and what is expected of them. Make new employees feel welcome – they need to know they are part of a group and have a "work family".

4. DEVELOPMENT INTERVENTIONS

Development interventions and training are required for any new employee. A blended learning approach is most effective. Most learning and development takes place on the job, in projects and during cross-functional learning, rather than in endless classes. Approximately 75% of learning should take place in the actual work situation: cross-functional projects and on-the-job training with colleagues and under supervision. The remaining 25% is "other" learning. This includes self-development, reading, research and a better understanding of the company in general. It can be classroom based or team-leader driven.

PART 3: LEADING THE TEAM

5. RELATIONSHIPS AND NETWORKING

New employees must be helped to understand the network of connections and relationships underlying the day-to-day functioning of the business. Team leaders should promote networking and encourage employees to have healthy relationships with colleagues. This creates a solid support structure that team members can turn to in times of difficulty.

6. RETENTION

Employees stay in a business because they are happy. If a person feels valued and respected at work, they don't feel that driving need to move on. Recognition, encouraging growth and promoting self-development are key factors in developing and retaining people and teams.

7. EXIT

The way a team leader handles an employee's exit says so much about the team and business culture. When it comes to headcount issues and downsizing, it is easy to focus on the figures and forget about the people behind the numbers. When headcount needs to be reduced, companies should ensure the process is carried out with compassion. If there is a need to terminate a team member's contract, it is essential it is done according to the book and with dignity and care.

"I think if leaders want to do anything, they need to encourage the workforce. When you hire somebody, they've got to have learnability. They have to be curious. Those are the people who are going to help change and work towards the future

"You can hire somebody who's brilliant and clever in that technical aspect you're looking for, but it's important to recognise that what we're looking for today is needed *today*, but it may not be five years from now, and definitely not 10 or 15 years from now.

"So, the number-one quality to be looking for in people is learnability. If leaders want to coach and lead their teams, they need to openly talk about learnability and look at learning and development solutions that encourage learnability, and make sure people realize their education's never going to be over."

Kris Kumfert
Chief Human Resources Officer, Clark Pacific
United States

PART 3: LEADING THE TEAM

8. LEAD BY TEACHING, COACHING, MENTORING AND ROLE-MODEL BEHAVIORS

Leaders have a wealth of knowledge and experience that, when shared, accelerates the growth and development of others. Transformational leaders educate and coach their teams. It is important you create plenty of formal and informal learning opportunities so the team can grow.

"Lunch and learns" are an easy and acceptable mode of training and development. Mentoring is also highly effective. A mentor is someone who shares their invaluable wisdom with someone who is entering their field. They guide, advise and help them focus on the right areas. Mentoring can involve members of your team and/or those of another. Transformational leaders make excellent mentors.

Coaching involves asking the right questions so the person finds their own answers. If team members can find their own answers, it will have a greater impact than if someone had simply told them what to think. In the process, they learn a lot about themselves, which is essential for development.

"I'm definitely big into the leadership team realizing we have to foster a learning environment. That means a lot of things. That means leaders are teachers and making sure they communicate that way.

"If ego is a concern, that's when I go back to the idea that leaders are teachers who are constantly curious and learning. If you get to a point that you really are committed to constantly learning and leading and coming up with ideas, you can't help but notice the fact you don't know everything. You can't help but notice that you walk away from certain articles, videos and interactions going, 'Huh, that makes a lot of sense. I never thought of it that way.'

"I think if you're feeding yourself a steady diet of that kind of thought of, 'I never thought of that. That's an interesting way that they framed that,' you just can't help but erase some of your ego and be a far more open leader."

Kris Kumfert
Chief Human Resources Officer, Clark Pacific
United States

THE EIGHT QUALITIES OF HIGHLY EFFECTIVE TEAMS

1. Understand the maturity level and lifecycle of the team.
2. Acceptance of deliverables and the drive to deliver.
3. Adopt effective problem-solving techniques.
4. Effective communication.
5. Inter-team recognition.
6. Respect for diversity.
7. Integrity.
8. Ownership, accountability and responsibility.

1. UNDERSTAND THE MATURITY LEVEL AND LIFECYCLE OF THE TEAM

A mature team is one that has been operating for a relatively long time. It's important that team members understand where they are in terms of their own maturity in the team, as well as the maturity of the team as a whole.

This is because there is a process for establishing a team. A team's lifecycle has many stages as members move from individuals to a cohesive group with common goals and aspirations. The stages of a team's development are explained by Dr Bruce Tuckman's "forming, storming, norming and performing" model, first published in 1965.[2] In the 1970s, he added a fifth stage known as the "adjourning stage". It is a highly useful model that explains how teams develop their maturity and ability.

Let's look at the five stages in greater detail.

2 "Forming, Storming, Norming, and Performing: Understanding the Stages of Team Formation," MindTools. https://www.mindtools.com/pages/article/newLDR_86.htm

- **Forming.** In this stage, team members are getting to know each other and their responsibilities. They look to the leader for guidance and direction. The leader is perceived as all-knowing. The leader's focus is often on "telling" members what to do as they learn their new roles.

- **Storming.** This is when team members start pushing the boundaries. They vie for positions while trying to establish themselves. Decisions do not come easily within the group. While the clarity of the group's purpose increases, uncertainties remain and there can be conflict between members' working styles. Cliques and factions form. The team must focus on its goals to avoid becoming distracted by relationships.

- **Norming.** Team members start to resolve their differences and become more united. They get to know one another better and learn to compromise. Agreements are formed, members develop a stronger commitment to the team and they respond well to facilitation by the leader.

- **Performing.** The team is now strategically aware and knows what it's doing. Members have a shared vision and work towards a common goal. Relationships are valued, processes are followed, and team members look out for each other. Disagreements can still occur, but conflict is handled positively. The team as a whole makes necessary changes to processes and structure. Now that the team leader can delegate on projects, he or she can concentrate on developing team members. It's important the leader doesn't return to a directive style of leadership. If this were to happen, the team could slip back to the forming stage.

- **Adjourning.** This relates to the breakup of the group. Once the task is successfully completed, the group can dissolve. People move on with a sense of achievement. From a company perspective, recognition should be given for the work accomplished.

2. ACCEPTANCE OF DELIVERABLES AND THE DRIVE TO DELIVER

A deliverable is something the team produces or provides. It defines what needs to be done. Deliverables must be agreed upon by all members of the team. It is not effective to have someone on the team who disagrees with what must be done. The team must feel accountable to the process.

Deliverables should also be measurable. What do you plan to achieve? What will be the outcome and what are the metrics?

3. ADOPT EFFECTIVE PROBLEM-SOLVING TECHNIQUES

Problem-solving techniques are crucial to a team's success. They offer step-by-step processes that enable the team to deal with what may seem insurmountable problems.

There are four steps to problem-solving:

1. Identify the issue.
2. Understand the data.
3. Find solutions.
4. Implement the solutions.

A team needs a strong governing structure to ensure these four steps are carried out. There are many problem-solving techniques available, such as the GROW model, root cause analysis, eight disciplines (8D) problem-solving process and the PDCA (plan, do, check and act) process, to name a few.

4. EFFECTIVE COMMUNICATION

Effective communication involves everyone in the team. It creates a safe space. When communication is open and encouraged, members feel comfortable enough to drop their defences and share issues of concern.

Trust is the basis here. Members must feel they can be open and honest about their feelings and opinions, trusting that their viewpoint will be respected and not judged.

Considered feedback between team members is another critical element of effective communication. It creates healthy relationships and gives people an objective view of a situation. When conflict does arise, it should always be dealt with in a mature and reasonable way.

5. INTER-TEAM RECOGNITION

Team members must recognize that not everyone is the same. Inter-team recognition is vital to great and lasting relationships. Recognize that each member has a different role. Some roles may be more complex, but each member must play their part and no one is more important than the other.

Recognition for contribution is also a must. The success of the team does not fall to just one person – it is the result of the contributions made by every member. Rather than singling people out, acknowledge the success of the team as an entire unit.

Furthermore, members must understand there are different levels of competency within the team. Some people may be relatively new, which means they need more help and support.

I HAVE YOUR BACK

Photographing zebras is easy – they are plentiful and, like most members of the horse family, highly sociable.

Certain species of zebra live in groups, known as "harems". These harems may consist of one stallion and up to six mares and their foals. Bachelor males live alone or with a group of other bachelors until they are old enough to challenge a breeding stallion.

When attacked, a group of zebra huddles together. They protect the foals in the middle while the stallion wards off the attackers. This group cohesiveness and togetherness is evident in many photos I have taken of zebras. They stand close to one another, resting their heads on each other's backs. They are comfortable together, choosing to be part of a group. This affords them a greater sense of safety.

Similarly, for a workgroup or team to function effectively, there must be a sense of trust between team members. Team members must be reliable, open, honest and accepting of one another. Having each other's back is essential to creating trusting relationships and group cohesiveness. Looking out for each other, protecting one another and offering assistance are essential.

To have each other's back means the following:

- **Commit to the team and yourself.** Deliver what you say you will and stay true to your word.
- **Help each other.** When a team member is in trouble, jump in and help. Offering support ensures their survival – and quite possibly your own.
- **Accept help when in trouble.** This is as important as offering help. To accept help means you trust your team members to act in your best interest.
- **Be respectful.** If a team member is not present in a conversation, do not speak badly of them. Defend fellow team members. Or, at the very least, postpone the conversation to a time when the team member is available to present their case and point of view.
- **Support is unconditional.** Team members should expect nothing in return when they help others.

In a high-functioning team, the default position is one of trust. Team members have each other's back, no matter what. The strength of the group lies in its unity.

PART 3: LEADING THE TEAM

6. RESPECT FOR DIVERSITY

Diversity is a core element of an effective team. Diversity may refer to any number of differences: age, gender, ethnicity, religion, disability, sexual orientation, education and natural origin.

We are all different in so many ways – some seen and some unseen. It is important for team members to not only recognise diversity but to respect it. This creates a culture of inclusivity, where people feel accepted and confident, boosting morale, performance and productivity. It also ensures the group encompasses a variety of skills, talents and experiences, which benefits the team and the organization.

7. INTEGRITY

Integrity refers to the basic values of the team. What does it stand for? What standards does it uphold? Do members truly believe in these standards and behave accordingly?

Trust, respect, non-judgment, reliability, appreciation and recognition are all values that speak of a team's integrity. To act with integrity means to act according to these values. When the team is challenged or under pressure, it is imperative it responds with its core values in mind. Otherwise, ethical failures can occur, which undermine team cohesiveness, trust, loyalty and productivity.

"As a leader, you need to capitalize on the good times and survive the tough times, which is an inevitable characteristic of the economic world. To be consistent in response and decision making, one needs to have a value system based on solid principles, which is indigenous yet in line with habits and values that drive long-term success.

"Some of the key values that I think are critical to being a good leader are the basic human values of humility, which to me is the absence of arrogance, and integrity, which is as simple as being really true to what you are doing, where you would like to reach and how you will get there.

"These values get tested the most when the going is too easy or really tough – easy success can make you pompous or over-confident, and tough times can tempt you to discard integrity, even if fleetingly so. These missteps may help you survive temporarily, but every wrong move is an erosion of your value system, which will undermine you as an individual and leader, and eventually as an organization."

Anilesh Kumar
CEO at Levtech Consulting, Director Development, Yegertek
United Arab Emirates

PART 3: LEADING THE TEAM

8. OWNERSHIP, ACCOUNTABILITY AND RESPONSIBILITY

We often talk about ownership of an issue. But what does it mean? It means we treat the business or situation as our own. We take responsibility for it. Every decision, every action and every outcome – good and bad – belong to all members of a team. Everyone is accountable and answerable to the issue.

When all members of a team take ownership of an issue, it removes the need to blame. It reinforces that all team members are "in it together", fostering a greater sense of comradeship and unity. It's also easier for the team to deal with the issue and find a way forward.

FOLLOW-THROUGH: THE ROADMAP TO INSIGHT IN TEAM EFFECTIVENESS

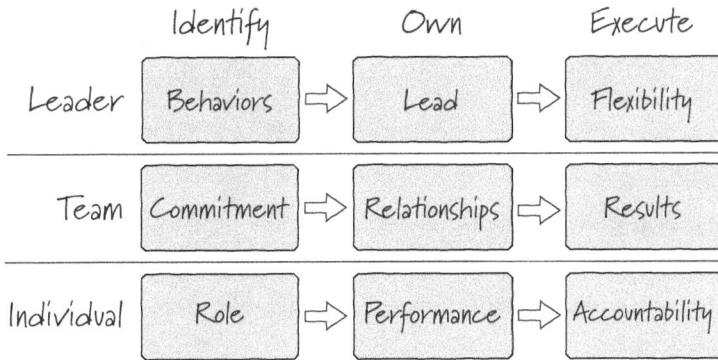

	Identify	Own	Execute
Leader	Behaviors ⇨	Lead ⇨	Flexibility
Team	Commitment ⇨	Relationships ⇨	Results
Individual	Role ⇨	Performance ⇨	Accountability

Insight means putting the strategic components of leading the team to work. The roadmap to successful execution is through a process of **identification**, **ownership** and **delivery (execution)** of nine team components:

LEADER

1. IDENTIFY BEHAVIORS

A team consists of three elements: the leader, individual members and the team. Each element exhibits different behaviors, depending on the situation and the maturity or stage of the team's lifecycle.

- **Self-identify.** Where do you stand in terms of the team? What is your level of maturity? What behaviors do you display and reflect within the team? Are you required to tell, sell, participate or delegate? Do you have the necessary flexibility depending on the stage of the team's lifecycle and maturity of team members?

- **Identify the maturity level of the individuals.** Are team members competent? Do they need more development? Do they need more training? You need to treat each team member accordingly, as they may be at different maturity levels.
- **The team.** What is the maturity level of the team? Is it in the forming, storming, norming or performing stage?

2. OWN THE LEAD

A good leader provides the team with a clear vision. It is ultimately up to the leader to set the team's course and ensure each member understands what needs to be accomplished. This involves:

- **Setting direction.** What does the team aim to achieve?
- **Effective communication.** This must be done regularly
- **Focus.** What is the team focusing on? Does the team understand the metrics? Is it delivering against those metrics?

3. EXECUTE FLEXIBILITY

To operate effectively in different situations, the team leader must be flexible in their approach and style. They must be adaptable and agile so they can work with different levels of people at different stages of maturity.

Being able to adjust to change is important. A transformational leader must have the ability to remain open and responsive to new suggestions and remain amicable in the process.

TEAM

4. IDENTIFIES COMMITMENT

What does the team commit to? The group must understand what it commits to, how and when. This includes a commitment to the organization and between individual members. The team achieves commitment through:

- **Trust.** When team members have mutual respect, their relationships are imbued with trust – trust that the team will deliver and that members will support one another.
- **Being reliable.** Team members depend on each other and the organization depends on the team to do what is required.
- **Being responsible.** Team members assume responsibility for themselves, their team, their leader and the organization.

5. OWNS THE RELATIONSHIPS

Relationships cannot be forced; they must be developed and nurtured. Building strong and enduring professional relationships is about understanding and developing a strong team culture. Know what the culture is, invest in it and contribute to its well-being. Culture is not a top-down approach. It depends on how members choose to work with each other.

Strong relationships are also built on the ability to handle conflict constructively. Co-operation is key. It is a give-and-take situation – not just give, and not just take.

SEVEN BEHAVIORS THAT BUILD STRONG RELATIONSHIPS

Strong relationships are based on seven essential building blocks. The team leader must encourage these behaviors, so the relationships can grow, nurture and improve.

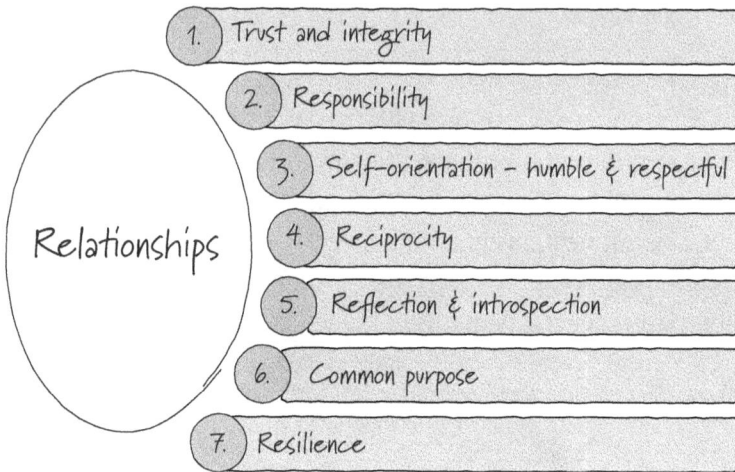

Relationships

1. Trust and integrity
2. Responsibility
3. Self-orientation – humble & respectful
4. Reciprocity
5. Reflection & introspection
6. Common purpose
7. Resilience

1. TRUST AND INTEGRITY

The team needs trust and integrity – between team members, and the leader and the team. Integrity is fundamental to team effectiveness – it goes hand in hand with a strong value system.

2. RESPONSIBILITY

The team must take ownership of what it does. This ensures there is no blame and no victim.

3. SELF-ORIENTATION – HUMBLE AND RESPECTFUL

Humility means not taking credit for everything. Every success is a team effort.

4. RECIPROCITY

This means giving back. It is in the giving that we often receive the most.

5. REFLECTION AND INTROSPECTION

These are important tools for personal growth. The team needs to regularly reflect on its performance, behaviors, achievements and areas of improvement.

6. COMMON PURPOSE

A common goal unites a team. Members need to know what they are working towards and that the goal is equally important for everyone in the team.

7. RESILIENCE

Good relationships require a resilient team leader and members. Resilience keeps the team together and on track during challenging times.

IT'S ALL IN OUR RELATIONSHIPS

Early one morning while on safari, we stumbled upon a family of spotted hyenas playing in the early morning sun. There were several males and females, as well as a few young in the pack. They were chasing each other, biting playfully, baring teeth and having a good time.

Watching them, they seemed happy. The family unit worked well. Everyone's role was defined and their relationships with one another were clearly understood.

The spotted hyena is native to sub-Saharan Africa and is a highly sociable animal. According to BBC Earth, they deserve a lot more respect and much less contempt from us humans. More often than not, they hunt their prey rather than scavenge. They are highly intelligent, with some of the largest group sizes and most complex social setups of any carnivores. The society is matriarchal and, at times, extremely competitive. The spotted hyena is regarded as a highly successful animal and its success is due, in part, to its adaptability and opportunism.

Strong relationships are a key component of every successful enterprise. Relationships built in the absence of mutual respect and trust become toxic, resulting in a lack of effective functioning. We all know how bad it is when personal or business relationships have no trust or respect.

The cornerstones of healthy relationships are:

- **Trust.** Trust is earned. It is created by the things we do. Trust is saying we will do something and doing it. Trust is being there for each other in times of need. Reliability and support are crucial to building and maintaining trust.
- **Integrity.** This is about being honest and truthful to yourself and others. Integrity is not a skill or a learned behavior – it is a choice. A healthy relationship is not possible without integrity.
- **Authenticity.** What you see is what you get. Be true to yourself. To be someone other than who you truly are is not being authentic or genuine.

Productive and healthy relationships are the cornerstones of personal well-being and effective business relationships. Like the hyenas, be competitive, but not destructive. Respect and understand the need for relationships. Good relationships make for good business.

6. EXECUTES RESULTS

Results are achieved through proper planning and execution over the long and short-term.

- Results are **developed** and **executed** through a plan that sets specific objectives for a period of time, i.e. goals for the next 12 months.
- Set a **specific target** against the objective.
- Set **metrics** against those targets.

INDIVIDUAL (TEAM MEMBER)

7. IDENTIFY YOUR ROLE – THE INDIVIDUAL IN THE POSITION

Primarily, we identify team members as having three roles: firstly, having a specific skill or expertise; secondly, having a personal obligation to the team as a team member; and thirdly, a responsibility to themselves as a person.

- A **subject matter expert** in their appointed position. The team relies on each member to develop their unique skill and competence.
- Each person has a certain **responsibility** to and **accountability** for the team.
- Team members are also **leaders** in and of their position.

8. OWN PERFORMANCE

Performance is not only about the result. Team member performance is also about:

- **Effort.** How hard did the individual try? How much energy and time did it take to deliver the result? Was it an honest effort?
- **Skill.** Team members must continually develop their skills and competence. Learning is a lifelong process.
- **Overall contribution.** How has each person contributed to the team? Was it the best they had to offer?

9. EXECUTES ACCOUNTABILITY

Individual team members hold themselves and others around them accountable for the results. In other words, they take responsibility for what the team delivers.

There are three levels of accountability:

- **Actions.** Purposeful steps move the team towards delivery.
- **Obligations.** Team members accept their role and what they are responsible for.
- **Assurance.** The individual is confident each member will deliver what is required.

THE IMPACT

Healthy, strong relationships are a key component of every successful team and enterprise. Relationships built in the absence of mutual respect and trust become toxic, resulting in a breakdown of effective team functioning. As a transformational leader, you must build your team on a solid foundation of trust, integrity and authenticity, and continue to nurture the team through its lifecycle.

The impact of team effectiveness is as follows:

Past	Future
Disengage ✗	Commitment ✓
Division ✗	Alignment ✓
Blame ✗	Accountability ✓
Victim ✗	Ownership ✓
Conflict ✗	Trust ✓

GREAT LEADERS IDENTIFY TALENT AND NURTURE IT INTO A POWERFUL FORCE.

LEADING THE BUSINESS

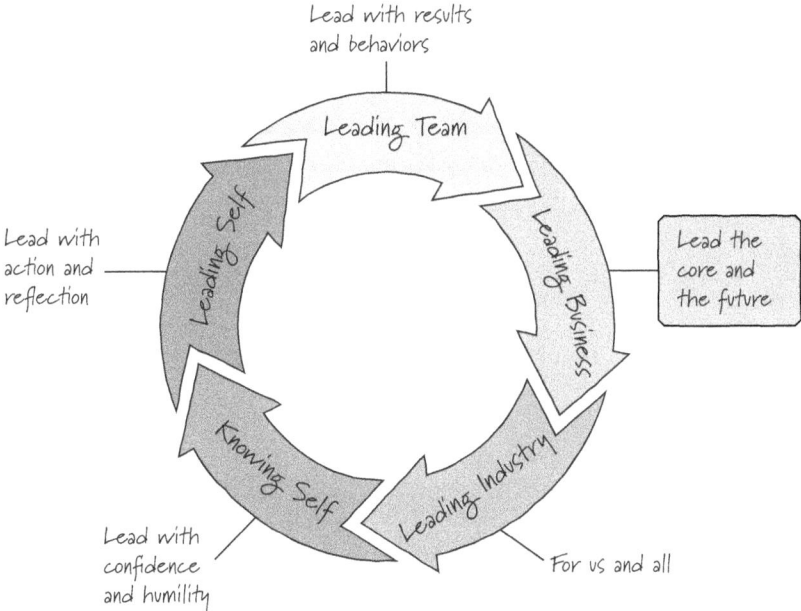

Lead with results and behaviors

Leading Team

Lead with action and reflection

Leading Self

Leading Business

Lead the core and the future

Knowing Self

Leading Industry

Lead with confidence and humility

For us and all

PART 4

LEADING THE BUSINESS: LEAD THE CORE BUSINESS AND BUILD THE FUTURE

A LEADER'S VIEW FROM THE TOP

Soaring 828 meters above Dubai, the Burj Khalifa is the world's tallest building. Designed by architectural firm Skidmore, Owings & Merrill (SOM), the 162-storey tower is a magnificent feat of engineering, and an opportunity to visit the tower should not be missed when visiting Dubai. From the viewing platform on the 124th floor, one can take a photo from the top looking down. It is breathtaking and seems like you are on top of the world!

I often think about the view leaders have. Being a senior leader requires courage and authenticity. Much has been written about authentic leadership and the leadership qualities that emerge when a company experiences serious challenges. This is when true-self leadership emerges.

PART 4: LEADING THE BUSINESS

Bill George, in his book *True North*, describes authentic leadership as leading with heart and passion. Indeed, some of the best leaders I have met lead with heart and passion – what you see is what you get.

The following qualities are essential in an authentic leader:

- **Values.** Great leaders know what their value system is. No matter the difficulty, they will not compromise their values, which include being truthful and having unquestionable integrity.
- **Mindful and self-aware.** Authentic leaders have excellent work-life management systems and take care of their whole person. Their approach is mindful – they are present when they engage. Their actions and decisions are deliberate and non-judgmental.
- **Long-term focus.** Authentic leaders are not focused on instant gratification or instant results. They are in it for the long haul and their decisions reflect this.
- **Compassion.** They understand the difference between compassion and empathy. They can identify when they need to help and do something constructive about another person's dilemma and suffering.
- **Teachable.** Authentic leaders understand the value of introspection and feedback. They remain teachable in their approach and are open to advice and constructive criticism.

The journey to the top can be daunting and sometimes hair-raising. But the view is inspiring and a reward in itself. From this place of privileged perspective, it's important you share your view and insights and do what you can to ensure the journey upwards of those around you.

"It almost feels like you're going to have to go back and build from the foundation of starting with what makes a good leader.

"In fact, when my daughter was six years old, we were sitting together and I was multi-tasking, writing and reading articles while she was playing around me. She peeped at what I was writing and read out loudly, 'Leadership.' I said, 'Oh, you read now.' She said, 'Yes, I do.'

"Then I asked her, 'Do you know what it means?' She said, 'I know what it means.'

"'Huh,' I said. 'OK. Tell me, who's a leader then?'

"She said, 'One who knows what is right and is not afraid to do it.'"

Kamali Rajesh
Head of Human Resources APAC, Syngenta Asia Pacific,
Singapore

STRATEGIC PERSPECTIVE: LEADING THE BUSINESS

RELATIONSHIP MODEL SUPPORTING LEADING THE BUSINESS

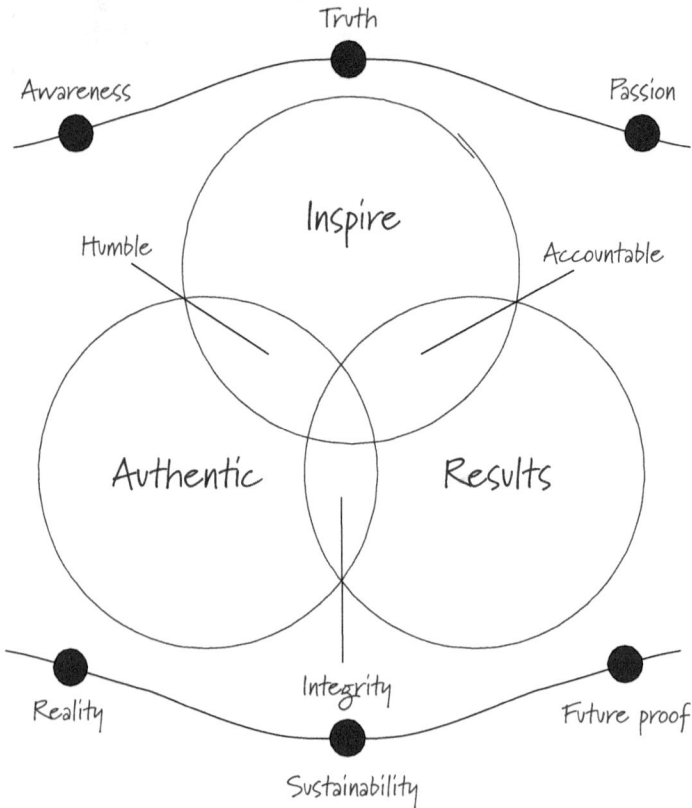

To gain a strategic perspective of leading the business, let's look at the three core components.

1. INSPIRE

Leaders need to inspire their teams and the business. It can be a lonely position at times, but leaders serve as a beacon and must motivate those around them.

There are three ways a leader can inspire:

- **Energize the team.** Motivate and energize people. Inspire them to have the necessary energy and drive.
- **Ignite people to action.** Your enthusiasm will be infectious, encouraging people to execute and stay the course.
- **Galvanize everyone around you.** Your inspiration will invigorate the team and organization. They will work together cohesively, which is what gets the results.

LEADERSHIP IS A LONELY JOB

The Cape Otway Lighthouse is Australia's most significant lighthouse. It was built in 1848 and is the oldest lighthouse on mainland Australia. It sits on towering cliffs 80 meters above where Bass Strait and the Southern Ocean collide.

For thousands of immigrants, Cape Otway was their first sight of land after leaving Europe and North America many months prior. The lamp was originally fueled by whale oil and shone 48km out to sea.

The sense of the past is so strong here, and there are numerous stories of ghosts. Many lives were lost in these dangerous seas. Think of the horror of the immigrants who survived the passage at sea, only to die as their ship wrecked at the end of their journey. Similarly, think about the relief and excitement of the sailors and new immigrants who finally saw the welcome beam, knowing land was near and a new adventure awaited.

Embarking on an international assignment outside your home country is a daunting task at best. Generally, the working spouse will arrive at the new destination first, navigating their way through a whole new world. After the first six months, the honeymoon period is over and reality sets in. The novelty of all things new wears off and the real task begins.

I remember my first assignment as a leader in an emerging market, where nothing I knew was the same. The people, the shops, the currency, the culture and the language –

everything had changed. As a senior leader, the expectation is to perform from day one and the demands are enormous. My main performance criteria were to grow the operation and teach and develop national talent. How do you survive and thrive in such a time of upheaval?

- **Inner strength.** Know who you are and where you draw your inner strength from. Understand what your strengths and weaknesses are as a leader.
- **Confidence in your abilities.** Self-confidence and a belief in your abilities are critical. The unexpected will happen and you must be ready and willing to deal with it.
- **Show the way.** Be the lighthouse. Light the way for others, even when the environment is just as unfamiliar for you. Overcome your fears to help and guide others.
- **Leader-teacher.** As an expat, you have two primary missions. The first is to grow your company. The second is to be a leader-teacher. This may be incredibly challenging, but the benefit of balancing the demands of being a leader and teacher is that you learn and grow alongside the people you mentor and guide.
- **Immerse yourself in the culture.** Rather than mixing with people you know, take the plunge and immerse yourself in the culture. Take day trips and visit local points of interest. Go away for a weekend and explore the region. Extend your boundaries and take the opportunity to better understand the culture. If you can, learn the language or at least master a few basic words. This will go a long way towards gaining acceptance and trust from the people in your new environment.

A lighthouse serves as a navigational aid for maritime pilots at sea or on inland waterways, marking dangerous coastlines, hazardous shoals, reefs and safe entries to harbors. As an expat leader, think of yourself as a lighthouse. It may be a lonely and challenging job, but without your guidance, it is easy for the less experienced to flounder and run aground in the perilous waters of unknown territory. You become a beacon of light for others, illuminating the way and guiding them to a place of safety.

In the words of James Michael Pratt in his book, *The Lighthouse Keeper*: "We have a light upon our house, and it gives hope to all who sail upon the stormy seas. Do you know what it means to have a light burning atop your home? It is safety, a place of refuge, seen by all as a signal that you stand for something greater than this world, greater than us all."

2. AUTHENTIC

Authentic leadership is based on three important elements: being trustworthy, dependable, and consistent.

- **Being trustworthy.** Your team and stakeholders know they can trust you to do the right thing. You have their best interests at heart. You look out for them and the future of the company is always at the forefront of your mind.
- **Being dependable.** You do what you say you will do. What you promise to deliver gets done. Being dependable means people consistently get the best from you. It also implies you are ready to be accountable and take responsibility for your business. You make no excuses for a lack of results. When people feel they can rely on you, whether it be stakeholders, your employees, customers or the community, they know that under any set of circumstances, you will not let them down.
- **Being consistent.** This important leadership attribute is often overlooked, but it can have an enormous impact on the organization over time. Inconsistency in leadership style and decision-making creates confusion and detracts from performance.

"I've been thinking about what attributes of leadership are changing. I've also been thinking about what attributes of leadership are not changing and won't change.

"I do think there are fundamentals of leadership that are timeless. For example, self-awareness. Whether it was 50 years ago, now, or 50 years from now, great leaders will always need to have strong self-awareness. 'How do I show up?' It doesn't matter how I perceive myself; it's how others perceive me. That, to me, doesn't change.

"Technology changes leadership, in the sense that I need to understand how I come across to others who are now communicating with me using a lot of different methodologies that were not available 50 years ago. There will also be different technologies in the future and we don't even know what they'll look like.

"I think leaders, past, present, future, always have to know how to inspire people. What inspires people, to me, is contextual. What inspires people in Detroit, Michigan, may be very different from what inspires people in London, Bangalore, Shanghai or Tokyo. How do I adjust or craft my messaging in a way that people, regardless of their contextual frame, will find inspiring and motivating?

"Then there are the basics. How do I give feedback to people? How do I respectfully challenge others? To me, there are things in that bucket that are fundamentals, and I really don't think they're different or have changed that significantly. And then there's the whole basket of things that are changing.

How do I manage my social media presence? These are issues that no leader had to think about, really, 15 or 20 years ago, and that's become infinitely more complicated."

David Everhart
Senior Vice President, Leaders & Talent at Mannaz A/S,
London, United Kingdom

3. RESULTS

When leading the business, delivering planned results is critical. Ultimately, this is the basis on which all leaders are judged. The results you deliver in terms of the vision, strategy and plan speak volumes. Results also reflect the level of confidence you have created with your customers and employees.

Delivering results requires focus in three areas:

- **Design and execute strategic priorities.** These priorities are a direct outflow of your strategy and vision.
- **Design and implement specific targets.** These give effect to the priorities.
- **Implementation of a robust governance process.** This process is designed to review the strategy, priorities and measurable targets. Its main aim is to track performance and execution.

PART 4: LEADING THE BUSINESS

Now, let's look at the three intersections of the relationship model supporting leading the business.

1. HUMILITY

A leader at this level should remain humble and respectful. These qualities reflect the difference between a transformational leader with influence and a leader whose focus is on power. Leading with power is to lead through position and titles. But leading with influence is to lead through impact and engagement.

Being respectful and leading with influence and humility require the following:

- **Ability to listen.** It is critical you listen to what people have to say. Ask questions and listen carefully to what your customers, employees, colleagues and stakeholders are saying. Listening provides you with different perspectives. Being open and receptive to other points of view you will help you make balanced and sound decisions.
- **Empathy.** This goes together with effective listening skills. It is the ability to put yourself in another person's position to get a better understanding of their circumstances. You must make the health and welfare of your employees, customers and stakeholders a priority.
- **Compassion.** To be compassionate means not only having empathy for someone else, but it's also the desire to help them. You purposefully try to make someone else's life easier by resolving some of their problems. Compassion goes a long way towards relieving some of the burdens people feel, which ultimately creates a healthier business environment.

"There are many examples of such failures across corporates and individuals, whether it's Arthur Andersen or Lance Armstrong. These big brands and high performers have failed eventually, after a long run of success, due to a breakdown of basic human values. Individuals of authority have made wrong decisions based on certain pressures and short-sighted short-term goals, and ultimately that has resulted in disaster.

"Therefore, I think young leaders need to espouse a strong sense of humility, ability to listen and learn, and stay the course for long-term success. As young leaders will increasingly work with teams that have people of diverse backgrounds and age groups, the one thing that really gets people together and removes any barriers that exist is humility – being nice and wearing a smile. In coming times, leaders will have to demonstrate a high amount of EQ consistently in the face of tough business decisions. I believe only a sound value system can help you navigate this dichotomy."

Anilesh Kumar
CEO at Levtech Consulting, Director Development, Yegertek
United Arab Emirates

2. ACCOUNTABILITY

As a business leader, you remain accountable and responsible for the results of the business – the profit, loss and future success. Accountability means you know the buck stops with you. As a transformational leader, you are accountable to:

- **Yourself.** What did you plan to achieve and what have you delivered? Be honest about your delivery. It is easy to find excuses, blame extenuating circumstance or even shift the blame to someone else. If the results are not delivered, you must take full ownership. Only you can create your legacy. What legacy do you want to leave for those who will follow you?
- **Your stakeholders.** These are typically the board of directors, your customers and other shareholders in the business.
- **The organization.** This includes the leadership team and the employees you serve.

3. INTEGRITY

We have previously discussed integrity in terms of the team. But what defines a senior leader's integrity? What do their people want to see in them?

- **Values.** Do you know what your values are? Do you uphold them no matter what? Does your business also have a clearly defined value system and does it stick to it? It is easy to compromise on values when you are under pressure or a quick short-term win could be gained. But compromising on values is never a good idea and may have long-lasting, negative repercussions.

- **Commitment.** Stick to the task. Senior executives often underestimate the amount of time, energy and oversight required to see a successful assignment or transformation process through. It is often far easier to design a strategy than it is to implement and execute it successfully. Commitment means staying on course despite difficulties and seeing the task through to completion.
- **Consistency.** Employees work well under a leader who is consistent. They appreciate consistency in decision-making processes, as they know what to expect and where they stand. Even if a decision is not popular or causes difficulty, the fact it is consistent will go a long way towards garnering employee support.

"To me, this is a key cornerstone of leadership, which is often not discussed, and that is the role of the leader to set moral and ethical standards. The one thing a leader needs to bring to their role is clarity. Everybody needs to be very clear on where they're steering the ship. That's not just around things like, 'Within five years, we are going to double our market share.' It's not just around metrics and dollars and units sold. I think a leader has to enunciate to everybody in the company, but potentially, everybody in society, what they want the company to stand for.

"They have to be clear on finding their north star and steer in that direction. When you have complete honesty and openness and transparency and fairness as to how everybody is treated, you don't compromise on those things. Even if it means lower profits that year, you don't compromise on those things. You don't say, 'Well, we actually had to hide that bit of information from shareholders because otherwise, our share price would have gone down.' There's no excuse for hiding the truth.

"Once you get into a leadership position, you have a platform to speak from. I think the most important people in society are nurses and school teachers and people like that, but for some reason, society bows at the altar of business leaders. The fact that they do places a big responsibility on every business leader to speak publicly about their position in regard to morals and ethics and societal injustices. Every business leader should be a warrior for social justice, as far as I'm concerned."

Dr David Cooke
Chairman and Managing Director, Konica Minolta Australia
Adjunct Professor, UTS Business School, Sydney, Australia

SIX THINGS GREAT LEADERS DO EVERY DAY

Executives are often dragged down by information overload. Vast amounts of email communication leave little time to think about strategy and future planning. Endless meetings and hours spent in airport lounges also steal valuable time for productivity. Fortunately, making a few small changes will make your life as a leader easier. It will also add value to the business.

1. BECOME TECH SAVVY

Be tech savvy beyond the normal company systems. Artificial intelligence (AI) and cognitive technologies are the new game changers. Leaders who are not prepared to embrace AI and its associated progress will be left behind. AI is no longer regarded as the future of the workplace – it is very much the present! It is happening all around us. AI will transform key dimensions of the business, and it is critical we embrace it. We will discuss the impact of AI in greater detail in Part 5 of this book.

2. INVEST TIME IN YOUR OWN LEARNING

How much of your "off" time do you spend learning? Limit your consumption of social media, as this is time generally lost with little worthwhile gain. Spend more time reading books and learning about new technology, methodologies and ideas. Expand your horizons. Ongoing self-education is the best investment. Also, remember to share what you have learned. By sharing your new thoughts and insights, you become a leader-teacher.

3. RUN TO THE FIRE

When you see a problem, find ways to provide whatever support is needed. Be innovative. Move away from utilizing traditional, more comfortable methods of problem-solving. A great leader will see challenges as opportunities to innovate and create. Take a calculated risk and run towards the fire.

4. GET TO KNOW THE WORLD OUTSIDE YOUR OFFICE

Senior leaders and executives are uniquely positioned, as they have a broad perspective of the entire organization. Why not use this opportunity to get to know everything about your business, including your people and the issues they face? Remember to step outside the confines of your office and genuinely get to know people.

5. BE COURAGEOUS – HAVE THOSE DIFFICULT CONVERSATIONS

At some point, every executive finds themselves in a situation where they are forced to take a stand. It takes great courage to have those difficult conversations. But without robust conversations, the organization – and, indeed, the leader – cannot grow. As a senior leader, it is your responsibility to initiate these discussions. If you do not, who will?

6. RECOGNIZE THE POTENTIAL IN YOUR POSITION

Do not play it safe. Everyone else does. Great leaders recognize that with their position comes great responsibility and opportunity. They put themselves squarely in the business. They counsel when decisions have potentially adverse consequences and are not afraid to be held accountable. It is easy to command and control from the vantage point of your title, but transformational leaders understand the difference between power and influence. Influence is far more sustainable and builds long-lasting credibility.

"A person with a high EQ is probably a better leader than a person with a high IQ. I believe emotional intelligence is super important for the progression of a young generation.

"It is further important for them to realize that it's not about power. Power can be taken from you at any time. You gain it today, you lose it tomorrow.

"If you manage to develop a reputation as a person with high emotional intelligence and a person who understands people on a different level, I believe you win favouritism quickly, and I don't think you can easily lose it, unless, once again, we go back to the ego state. If you fall into an ego state, the possibility of undoing all your work is strong, but otherwise, if you haven't and your emotional intelligence remains high, I believe you'll be a leader that can find the future."

Craig Siepman
CEO, Geotech Aviation South Africa
Johannesburg, South Africa

IMPROVING BUSINESS RESULTS THROUGH INNOVATIVE ENGAGEMENT

Leaders must inspire their teams to use creativity and innovation. They are key to business expansion and success. Generating excitement about innovation and creativity requires a calculated and determined process. This is because more often than not, innovation and creativity as a change process fail due to a lack of process and management effort.

Corporate transformations have a miserable success rate.[1] In fact, studies have shown that about 75% of change efforts fail. They fail to deliver the anticipated benefits or are abandoned altogether.

Flawed implementation and bad execution are often to blame for such failures. Analysis shows that misdiagnosis is equally to blame. Often, organizations pursue the wrong changes and in a fast-moving business world, it is easy to make the wrong choices.

Furthermore, organizations commonly fail to spend the time and energy to identify and drive alternatives. An analysis of 137 key decisions in as many North American companies found that when only one course of action was considered, 52% of the decisions resulted in failure.[2] By contrast, when just one alternative had been considered, the failure rate dropped to 32%.

1 N. Anand and Jean-Louis Barsoux. "What Everyone Gets Wrong About Change Management," *Harvard Business Review*, November-December 2017. https://hbr.org/2017/11/what-everyone-gets-wrong-about-change-management

2 Freek Vermeulen and Niro Sivanathan. "Stop Doubling Down on Your Failing Strategy," *Harvard Business Review*, November-December 2017. https://hbr.org/2017/11/stop-doubling-down-on-your-failing-strategy

"I firmly believe that innovation and change are not technical things. They are not techniques, they are not procedures, they are not projects. Innovation is an attitude. And that is what I try to give to people.

"Innovation is a way of thinking, wanting to change things all the time. If you see the possibility, even the slightest possibility to do something better, to make something more efficient, you have to do it. And it's not a program and it's not a book and it's not a movie, it is an attitude."

Dominique Michael Bellemans
CEO, Tera Vera Group

"Leaders are wired to think. Universities and all types of organizations, the government sector, the public sector in particular, because they are the biggest employers, must focus on encouraging people to see themselves as leaders and to behave as leaders. It is one thing to have this notion of self: that I'm a leader. But then deploying the leadership behaviors is another thing.

"One example is stewardship. The other one is owning the problem and owning the solution. So, if I display those types of attributes, then innovation and creativity will be natural consequences. It will be like night following day."

Gary W. Paul
Deputy Vice Chancellor, Resources and Operations, Central University of Technology, Free State, South Africa

BUSINESS REALITY

Against a background of significant business change, market headwinds, regional instability, business-model disruption and a push to increase market share, businesses are confronted with several realities:

- There are substantial costs and market pressure within the business model.
- There is an urgent requirement to deliver results over the short term and set the business over the long term.
- Change management has a poor success rate.
- Executing change management effectively remains elusive.
- Change management often occurs in "silos" within the organization, and the overall impact is low.
- Business models are disrupted by innovation.
- Due to stakeholder and market pressure, a problem/solution decision-making process is the preferred option, with varying degrees of success.
- It is necessary to develop a cohesive, high-performance organizational culture that embraces innovation, risks and opportunities.

"I have an answer to that (on facilitating creativity and innovation). I have to take you back to a marketing example, which is very interesting and it can be applied in this instance.

"I think this was 15 years back. There was a new global head of marketing for a large multinational. Like all new marketing people, the first thing they did was attack the agency and said the agency should do a better job. It's so easy to say that, right? Everybody has a view on advertising. My daughter has a view on advertising. My father has a view on advertising. Everybody will look at an ad and say, 'This car should have been white,' or, 'There should be no trees in the background.' It's such an easy subject to make a comment on. So, this guy makes the usual criticism at the agency and says, 'I want my marketing to be different. I really want it to be creative.'

"Everybody says those words, but what do they actually mean? So, the head of the agency at that point in time said, 'OK, give us a week and we will come back.' They go out for golf and then come back in a week and this guy expects a big presentation. They don't have a big presentation. They had one slide and the slide simply says, 'Our biggest problem is not being creative, as we can be as creative as required, but we rarely find clients who are willing to allow us to be that creative because they have a business to run.' So the agency said, 'We have a suggestion. If you agree to this, we will be creative.' And the head of marketing said, 'OK, what is it?'

"The agency proceeded to lay out their suggestion to the head of marketing: 'Look, I know that as the head of global marketing, you need to hit your monthly targets. We will take

70% of your budget and put it into very traditional classical media where we know we will get results. And that will make sure your short-term issues, like hitting your monthly targets, are achieved. Then we'll take another 20% of your budget and put it into what we call new media. (In those days Facebook, Google, all this was new media). We will take 20% of your budget and put it in new media because the world is changing, and we have to be aligned with that change.'

"That's 90% of the budget gone. Then the agency proposed, 'The rest – 10%, don't ask us any questions. Every quarter, we will use this 10% to do what we want, don't ask us questions. Maybe nine out of these 10 things we do every quarter with this 10% may fail, but give us the freedom to go and do it.' And this company said yes. So, that's what they did.

"I think companies have to take a similar approach where every year, they spend a certain amount of money on their basics. Because if you don't live to deliver this month's numbers and this quarter's numbers, there is no tolerance from the shareholders and stakeholders.

"I think CEOs probably need to follow a similar thing where they put 70% to 80% of their resources on the classical model because that's what keeps the shareholders happy, the business running and it takes care of the baggage. And maybe 10% or 15%, they have to look at what I would call 'great bets', which are not fully black, not fully white, but things like autonomous vehicles for automotive. Then you need to put some amount of resource – whether it's people or whether it's money or whether it's time – into something completely different. And you have to give them the freedom, unshackle them from their normal day-to-day affairs and let them really go and look at how they can be disruptive to the industry.

"I think that model is good, but I think for most CEOs, the struggle is to sell this kind of thing to the board. Because if the company makes, say, $10 billion a year, to go and tell the board, 'I'm going to now take $1 billion and put it on something that could be completely lost,' it is not an easy sell. It is much easier to say, 'I'll deliver your 1% market share growth, give me a half-a-million-dollar bonus.' It's not only risk; it's risk outside your classical model. If you have a traditional approach, they will apply the traditional tools of measuring the performance and they will not allow the model to work.

"So, the model has to not only be able to take risk but it also has to be outside the scope of your traditional metrics. Because that's what really kills the creativity. There's no point in saying, 'Can I have $1 billion to take an innovative approach?' The first thing the bureaucracy would say is, 'Show me the returns. Show me this, show me that.' You know, 'I want to sign off every coffee you buy.' And then this becomes another department of the company. You carry the same issues that have got you here into there."

Kalyana Sivagnanam
President, Nissan Motor Corporation
Regional Vice President for Africa, Middle East and India
United Arab Emirates

INNOVATIVE ENGAGEMENT: GENERATING EXCITEMENT AROUND CREATIVITY AND INNOVATION

Engaged with innovation	Business impact	% Brand engagement	% Business & people metric improvement
Excited	Exponential	80+	30
Committed	Expanding	60	20
Engaged	Stable	50	10
Tolerate	Stagnate	30	0
Disengaged	Contract	10	0

Business results can be significantly improved through innovative engagement. But for innovative engagement to work, leaders must take a strategic, process-driven approach. If they don't, they fall victim to the following five fatal transformation flaws:

1. Follow a problem-solution and/or action-recommendation approach.
2. Misdiagnose the problem and fail to seek viable alternatives.
3. Lack of cross-functional engagement to drive accountability and responsibility.
4. Inadequate tools to deliver solutions.
5. Lack of appreciation of the effort required to execute the plan.

"This is something very close to my heart. I'm an engineer and proud of it, so I'm attracted financially to innovation. But when you have a multicultural workforce like mine, you first of all have to slow down to go fast. You have to explain to them, what do you mean by innovation? Because for some, innovation is interpreted as invention. And you have to first of all distinguish in your own mind what is the difference between invention and innovation? What I often say to people is, 'I am not asking you to invent a mousetrap, OK? That's been invented already. But let's see how we could innovate a mouse trap. For example, we could make it cheaper. We could make it lighter. We could make it a more efficient killing machine. We could make it recyclable. We could make it perhaps a more pleasant experience for the mouse, etc.' This is what we'd call innovating on an existing process.

"And in a service industry like ours, I have an alternative definition of innovation, which is, *innovation is that force that acts against declining margins*. Think about that for a moment. Innovation is that force that acts against declining margins. If you were in a low-margin business that makes 4% net margin, I want you to tell me what you can do in your business processes and the way in which you execute your work to make that margin 5%. What can you do more efficiently, smarter, quicker, leaner so the margin goes up?

"Whatever ideas you have, I'm going to label them as innovative ideas. That is different from the way we used to do it. And it's giving me a bottom-line return. And so we have innovation awards in the company, where we reward people for some of the innovative things they've come up

PART 4: LEADING THE BUSINESS

with. And they've covered a broad range of things. Some
of them are simply business process improvements where
something is done much quicker than it was before. Others
have led to margin improvement by laying off people. These
small increments are vital. When you add them all up, if every
contract makes 1% increment on their margin, the collective
aggregate impact of that is huge. I mean huge.

"Now, I don't want them just to think about innovation at
that humble level. I'm also trying to get them to move up the
value chain and come up with innovative solutions in those
offerings we make to clients. For example, we go into an
airport where we get charged for looking after a thousand
assets at the airport. They give us an asset register and you
get read assets listed from A1 to 100, B1 to 100, C1 to 100,
etc. So, they want fast response times. I say to my guys,
'You know, we can use drawings and we can make one team
responsible for A1 to 100, and another team responsible for
B1 to 100, but what if we were really innovative?' Imagine
we've got ourselves a smartwatch and in this smartwatch,
we could code in the location and the GPS coordinates of
every asset on the watch. Then, if there's a downtime failure, a
buzzer would go off on an operator's watch arm and it would
tell him how many meters he was away from that asset, and
he could immediately go to that location. And when he gets to
that location, the problem could pop up on his watch and tell
him what to do. Now that's innovative."

David Greer, OBE, FIMechE
CEO, Serco Middle East, Africa and India
Executive Committee Member of Serco Group

INITIATING INNOVATION AND CREATIVITY

It makes business sense to implement an innovative engagement process. This must involve the whole leadership team. An innovative engagement process is designed to obtain collaboration from the entire executive team or stakeholder basis to develop creative ideas, understand the data, set priorities and hold the team accountable for delivery. In addition, it entrusts leaders with the responsibility of providing the tools required for delivery.

The innovative engagement process should focus on:

- Investing time and energy in creatively identifying and driving alternatives.
- Collaboration, which drives accountability and responsibility.
- Common priorities: act on maximum impact and high pay-back.
- Identification of tools required to deliver alternatives.

"In a previous role, I was tasked to create new businesses and/or product offerings that could ultimately be attached to an existing service line within the company. In my first year, nine out of 10 businesses that we presented were blocked by the firm's risk and compliance team. This was unsustainable from an ROI perspective. We quickly worked out that the risk and compliance team's KPIs were to not expose the business to any risk and, therefore, this had an unintended consequence of stopping new ideas from going to market. It was easier to maintain the status quo by saying, 'No.'

"To solve the conflict, we sat down and worked out a set of KPIs that operated within their risk and compliance framework, but incentivized the team for the number of opportunities that we jointly agreed could go to market.

"That subtle change is how I approach all my discussions. 'Don't tell me how it can't be done, tell me how you think it can be done.' Think about it from all sides, come up with a solution. It might not be the right one, but by approaching it with a solution mindset on how it could work, you end up building on the ideas and, ultimately, finding a solution that is typically better than the one you started with. It is more robust in terms of where it could fail, how you should build it and take it to market."

Andre Hugo
CEO, Virgin Money
South Africa

THE FOUR-STEP SUSTAINABLE AND REPEATABLE PROCESS

1. Facilitate the organization to identify the issue in its entirety. What is the issue you need to solve? What is the business opportunity? What is the burning platform?
2. Once the problem is well-defined, the next phase is to collect data. This phase is intended to inform the team's actions rather than affirm them.
3. With the data on the table, the next step is to make an informed list of solution alternatives.
4. With a solid solution, which is based on data and rooted in the originating business case, the team is well positioned for the final phase of implementing the change.

WHY YOU SHOULD ASK YOUR EMPLOYEES TO ALWAYS MAKE NEW MISTAKES

When profits are under pressure and markets are depressed, CEOs and executives typically have one concern: how to fix the business model and get better options and solutions – fast. This means organizations often pursue the wrong changes and make the wrong choices.

It is critical that executive teams figure out not only what to change, but what to change first – to prioritize. It is often because of the perceived risk of having to move outside one's comfort zone, or even a lack of trust in people within the organization, that not enough alternatives are pursued.

Many years ago, I was asked to take on a challenging and highly demanding position. My mentor at the time gave me an extraordinary gift. She handed me a card to pin on my whiteboard, which said: "Always make new mistakes." This left an indelible impression on me. It is only through going outside our comfort zone and taking risks that we learn and grow! Often, we will encounter resistance and challenges, but by persevering, putting ourselves out there and stretching ourselves to the limit, we find out just how far we can go.

One afternoon, standing on the windy cliffs overlooking a stormy Walker Bay in South Africa, I noticed an opening in the thick cloud through which the sun streamed. This brought to mind the late Leonard Cohen song, "Anthem". In it, he sings,

There is a crack in everything, that's how the light gets in.

In other words, nothing wonderful is perfect. It is the flaw that makes us unique, and it is the flaw that is the mark of human inspiration. We may not always succeed, but we are nothing if we have not tried.

There is a 500-year-old Japanese art form called "kintsugi". It is the art of recognizing the beauty in broken things. Kintsugi is the method of restoring a broken piece of porcelain with lacquer mixed with gold. This art elicits feelings of awe and reverence through restoration. The gold-filled cracks are a testament to the history of the piece. The kintsugi craftsman would say, "It is one beautiful way of living, that you fix your dish by yourself."

Great leaders give their people space and time to grow. They encourage them to take risks and think outside the square. They also allow and encourage employees to make new mistakes as they develop and support the business. Sometimes cracks appear and fixing is required. This is all accepted as part of the growth process.

What are the key actions of great leaders who support organizational growth and people development? They:

- **Encourage risk.** These leaders encourage employees to be innovative and take risks. They give them stretch assignments rather than prescribe every move and step. It is in the participation and delegation that bright and new ideas are born.

- **Provide a safety net.** When employees are encouraged to take risks, they are bound to make mistakes. It is a natural part of the process. What is their safety net? Do they get help? Are they supported or are they penalized for their mistakes? Chastising people for making mistakes is a sure way of stopping innovation and risk-taking.
- **Listen and give feedback.** Regular coaching and feedback are crucial to the development process. Listen, provide support and give feedback. Remember, this is a two-way process. A good leader does not tell people what to do – they question, ask for ideas and stimulate thoughts.

FOLLOW-THROUGH: THE ROADMAP TO LEADING THE BUSINESS

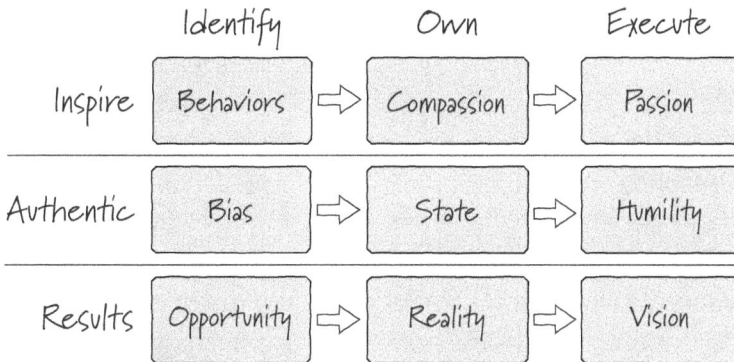

	Identify	Own	Execute
Inspire	Behaviors ⇨	Compassion ⇨	Passion
Authentic	Bias ⇨	State ⇨	Humility
Results	Opportunity ⇨	Reality ⇨	Vision

Insight means putting the tactical components of leadership for the business to work. The roadmap to successful execution is through a process of **identification**, **ownership** and **delivery (execution)** of the nine leading the business components:

INSPIRE

1. IDENTIFY BEHAVIORS

At this level, it is your state of mind that matters. How do you turn up every day? What is your attitude? How do others experience you? Do you recognise your behavior – what and how you say things, and what you do? It is crucial you are aware of your everyday behavior towards your team and customers. Behavior is defined by the following:

- **Attitude.** What's your attitude towards your responsibilities? Do you view what needs to be done as just another task, or do you take a considered approach? Do you bring your best version to the business every day?

- **Being** (you) as opposed to doing. The quality of leadership you bring to the organization is more important than your specific competency to do a task. Are you at peace with yourself and what you're doing? Being is a critical part of leadership. It is your attitude, what you bring to work, and it's a decision you make about how you turn up, treat others and how you treat yourself.
- **Presence.** Your behavior affects your presence. How do you make people feel when they work with you? How do they feel talking to you? How do they feel about the way you present yourself? Do you stay in your office and meetings most of the day, or do you walk around and make a point of interacting and getting to know others in the company?

2. OWN COMPASSION

Remember, leading with compassion implies not only that you have the required empathy, but that you purposefully try to resolve some of the problems people face. To actively apply compassion:

- **Look for ways to offer help and support.** When you are in touch with your employees, it is so much easier to be aware of situations requiring your intervention and assistance.
- **Actively do something to resolve the issue.** I remember as a young manager, a senior director once said his primary task was to remove roadblocks for people. This made an enormous impression on me. One would think that at that level, a senior executive would delegate and get other people to do things for them. It was so refreshing to think that someone at that level would use their seniority in the company not so much to command, but to help.

- **Circle back.** It's not good enough to simply provide help and forget about it. Follow up to see whether your assistance did, in fact, resolve the issue. Is there anything else that needs to be done? Employees place significant value on a senior executive who takes the trouble to come back and ask, "Has this issue been resolved? Is there something else I can do to help?"

3. EXECUTE PASSION

The best way to achieve a sense of fulfilment and accomplishment is to follow your passion. It energizes and motivates you to do more. This is what you must bring to the table when you are at this level – passion for what you do, how you treat others and your role. Passion is seen in a leader through:

- **High energy levels.** You can see a passionate person is energized. They solve problems, help people and take the company forward. Their energy is visible and contagious. They energize everyone around them. Passionate leaders are often prepared to take the biggest risks, push the business and take the industry forward.
- **Enthusiasm for success.** Passionate leaders are enthusiastic about helping others. They are excited to do what needs to be done for the business to succeed. This enthusiasm is highly infectious and motivates others.
- **Obsession to succeed.** A passionate leader is focused not only on making the company successful, but a better place for its employees. When you have the necessary energy, enthusiasm and obsession, that's when you hear people say, "That leader has a real passion for what they do – I can see it."

"Am I playing to win or am I playing not to lose as a leader? Based on my predisposition state, whether I'm in the game to win or I'm in the game not to lose, these two can bring in a very different approach and energy, which influences my change appetite, my risk appetite and my ability to energize people, rather than send a stream of fear into the system.

"There's a number of different variables that can come into play depending on what is my predispositions a leader. I have seen, and I continue to see, leaders who clearly want to win. There is no fear in their mind, they just jump into their work. There is a gleam in their eyes. There is so much energy in the way they want to influence. Their commitment to purpose is absolutely clear and unshakable.

"However, I also see people who are in the game, playing the game, so they don't lose. When you don't want to lose, you're not focused on the prize, you're focused on your face value. You're focused on avoidance so that it's clear in the system that the stress builds. They're not able to energize the people around them, they're stressing everybody out. Their commitment to purpose is diluted. So, it's a very different predisposition that a leader takes. I know it might sound a bit clichéd when I say a winning mentality, or a growth mentality, an abundant mentality versus a scarcity mentality, but it makes a real difference. Mentality counts."

Kamali Rajesh
Head of Human Resources APAC , Syngenta Asia Pacific
Singapore

AUTHENTICITY

4. IDENTIFY YOUR BIASES

No one can honestly say they are without bias or prejudice. It's important you're aware of these shortcomings and understand how they could potentially impact your judgment.

- **Question your status quo.** Step outside your comfort zone to ask, "Why?" and "What if?" Even if someone is dealing with a situation you are familiar with, it is always a good idea to ask yourself "why and what if" to identify and question your biases. You may discover you have an unintentional prejudice about what may have given rise to the issue or even how to solve the problem. This gives you an opportunity to change your mindset, as you may realize a different solution is needed.
- **Seek alternatives.** There are always other options or opportunities. There could be a variety of ways to solve a problem that are not immediately apparent.
- **Seek diversity.** When determining a strategy or plan, get a range of views and opinions. Encouraging diversity ensures you do not create a situation where you fall into comfortable, stale decision-making habits with similar outcomes.

"You learn from others, through others, through formal and informal learning, and, as a consequence, you become more self-aware. Make efforts to enhance your intuitive wisdom. Make efforts to become more aware of what exists in the realm of your own and others' unconscious and subconscious faculties. Because therein lies some of the untested and undiscovered truths about self and life. The more we delve into the things that are not obvious, the more we discover things that are great. So, that's a broad exposition on how leaders must be willing to continue to grow their thought patterns.

"I think the next thing that will make leaders successful is to demonstrate trust in those they deem to be their followers. Because I'm potentially putting my own success in your hands if you are my follower, I am required to trust you. To engender trust, I must be authentic as a leader. I must value others. I must encourage people's willingness to do new things, to take chances, to be willing to fail. And not to be suppressed by the fear of failure."

Gary W. Paul
Deputy Vice Chancellor, Resources and Operations,
Central University of Technology, Free State
South Africa

5. OWN YOUR STATE

Your state refers to how you feel about your happiness, your success and yourself. It is your state of being, which accompanies you to work every day. It is not necessarily an outcome of something outside yourself and beyond your control – it is a conscious decision about how you want to be, feel and behave.

Others experience your state of being in three main ways:

- **Perspective.** Your view of life and situations determines your outlook. A perspective is generally formed according to your past experiences and is unique to you.
- **Approach.** Are you a learning-teaching leader or are you a dictating leader? Are you approachable or distant and aggressive? It is important to know what kind of approach you adopt with people and in situations. Your state of being has a direct effect on your approach.
- **Attitude.** Your attitude influences your employees and the business in general. What is your attitude towards your people, shareholders and customers? Is it one of optimism and can-do?

6. EXECUTE HUMILITY

Your ability to be humble has a direct impact on the culture of your organization. Culture determines how people choose to work with each other. The ideal culture is based on mutual respect, dignity and inclusiveness. Leaders with humility create the right foundation for this type of culture.

"Every day, I invite any member of my staff to come to me and have tea at three. So, tea at three, you can come in for a cup of tea with the CEO. We talk about anything. And in that process, I've discovered extraordinary people and helped solve some of their problems that seemed insurmountable to them.

"These things are so humbling. I realize at my position, I have the power, the positive power, I should say, to help these people out of difficult situations. And you need a big heart as well and a sense of care to look after people. These kinds of experiences certainly keep me humbled and keep my feet firmly on the ground. If I did see anybody acting cockily and/or being too high for their station, frankly, I'd have no hesitation in telling them.

"Once a month or two times a month, I have a session called 'walk with the CEO'. Anybody who wants to come for a high, hard walk along the beach with me at 7.30 in the morning can join me. And I've had hordes of people. I get 40 or 50 people of all cultures – Indians, Pakistanis, Filipinos – all come out to be alongside the CEO so you can show them that you're just human. You've got the same things inside your body that they've got. You've got the same organs, the same fears, the same passions, the same worries about your kids and family. And when you show that humbleness to people, you do get extraordinary feedback from them.

"I think that my feet are very much on the ground in that regard. As a result, we have the highest staff engagement scores and people often ask me, 'How do you do it?' It's not through my day-to-day running of the business; it's the influence and the impact of all of these small experiences with people, some element of engagement with people of all walks of life that gets you these positive scores.

"One of my personal passions is photography. I love photography. It's the ability to freeze a moment in time. And it's there forevermore. And what I'm currently doing after hours is I run a photography club. We call it the 'click club'. Anyone in the company can join me in the click club, either on a call or face to face at the office. Through that, I introduced photography. Forget the fact that I'm the CEO – see me as a fellow photographer.

"And so, in this group, there's about 45 people now. We have 45 photographers of all different grades. Some with an iPhone, some with a Galaxy, some with a Canon, some with a Nikon, who are all now working together in this competitive way because we organize these little competitions once a month where people can put in their work. What I get out of that is a significant level of engagement and influence, while at the same time getting a bit of pleasure by pursuing one of my hobbies out of office hours."

David Greer, OBE, FIMechE
CEO, Serco Middle East, Africa and India
Executive Committee Member of Serco Group

A CULTURE OF MUTUAL RESPECT

I start my day with a walk at sunrise. It is a quiet and contemplative time, giving me an opportunity to witness the start of a new day filled with potential. I never walk without my camera in hand, and it was on just such a walk that I was able to capture a photo of a cleaner, picking up litter from a Dubai beach, with the downtown skyline in the background.

It made me think a lot about who we are as people. How do we behave? How is a corporate culture developed and nurtured? Here was a man, a simple cleaner, doing what most would regard as low-paid manual work, picking up litter with the glitz and glamour of modern Dubai in the background. I wondered what he must think about the people living in the upmarket high rises, with expensive cars and well-paid jobs? Then I thought about all of us living a privileged life in Dubai. How many of us ever really think about the less privileged?

This photo speaks to me about our unique roles in life. Do we take what we have for granted or do we approach life with gratitude and humility? Do we treat others with dignity and respect regardless of their position? We all have our roles in life. Some of us are cleaners, some supervisors and some CEOs. Do we see the person behind the position?

Respect, trust, dignity and a feeling of safety go to the heart of a company's culture. In their ground-breaking book *Everybody Matters*, Bob Chapman, CEO of Barry-Wehmiller, and Raj Sisodia tell the story of what happens when ordinary people discard long-accepted management practices and start operating from their deepest sense of right, with a sense of profound responsibility for the lives entrusted to them.

During the Great Recession, Barry-Wehmiller, like most other companies, faced severe challenges that could have been dealt with by sacrificing people for the benefit of the business. Instead, Chapman says, "We challenged ourselves with this question: How can we redefine success and measure it by the way we touch the lives of all our people? At the heart of our stories is a simple, powerful, transformative, and testable idea: Every one of our team members is important and worthy of care. Every one of them is instrumental in the future of our business, and our business is instrumental in their lives."[3] As a result, Barry-Wehmiller emerged from the downturn a stronger company with higher employee morale.

As leaders, we must keep in mind the following when we think about developing our corporate culture:

- **What is culture?** Culture encompasses the values, beliefs, traditions and behaviors of an organization and its employees. It permeates everything we do and say to each other. Culture is created, not designated, and we either like the culture or decide it is not what we signed up for.
- **Practice gratitude.** Gratitude helps us be mindful of what we have. Being grateful teaches us awareness, empathy and compassion. It allows us to see another person's situation so we can assist when help is needed.

---

3 Bob Chapman and Raj Sisodia, *Everybody Matters: The Extraordinary Power of Caring For Your People Like Family*, UK: Penguin Books, 2016.

- **Respect.** Treat yourself and others with respect and dignity. Do not judge a person by their material standing or position. Treat people the same way you want to be treated.
- **Reward, recognize and appreciate.** These are essential elements of a successful culture. They celebrate success and acknowledge good performance. Find ways to simply say "thank you". This is a powerful way for leaders to improve employee engagement and retention. In the words of leadership expert Simon Sinek, "When people are financially invested, they want a return. When people are emotionally invested, they want to contribute."
- **Everyone has a role.** We each have a unique role. Cleaners make the world a better place for us to be in, while CEOs have the great responsibility of running a company. Each is as important as the other.

Make time in your day to appreciate the people around you. Everyone is entitled to respect and dignity. Treat others as you want to be treated. This is what culture is all about. As the authors of *Everybody Matters* put it, "Everyone wants to do better. Trust them. Leaders are everywhere. Find them. People achieve good things, big and small, every day. Celebrate them. Some people wish things were different. Listen to them. Everybody matters. Show them."

RESULTS

7. IDENTIFY OPPORTUNITY

Operating results are the specific outcomes of priorities and goals that were defined, implemented and executed.

- **Additional opportunities.** Sometimes our results are not quite what we aimed for or expected. Rather than accept the result and move on, look to what other opportunities may exist. What could have been done differently? What could be improved?
- **Identify alternatives.** Are there alternatives you haven't considered?
- **Focus on strengths in your operating results.** These are aspects the company has excelled in. It is easy to focus on mistakes and spend an inordinate amount of time on analysis. You need to understand where mistakes were made, but don't let them detract from the obvious strengths. Accept mistakes were made and move on. Strengths can be leveraged, but mistakes should not be repeated.

8. OWN YOUR REALITY

The eyes through which you see the world determine the shape of your reality. How you choose to view life and the world around you determines whether your reality is one of opportunities and challenges or difficulties and problems. Own that reality but know you can change it. We often talk about the reality of a situation, but in truth, that reality is just your own. Someone else might have a completely different reality. A good leader stands back to think about their reality in a different way. Ask yourself, "Is this really so? Is it a fact or just my interpretation? How do I know this?"

9. EXECUTE A VISION

A vision is only viable and operational if you deliver against it. The ability to give your vision operational life depends on certain actions. These are:

- **Clarity.** Be clear about your vision. Visualize success. What does the outcome look like?
- **Develop your strategy.** Ensure it supports your vision and what you have set out to achieve. Does it reflect your idea of what success looks like?
- **Execute the strategy.** This must be done through priorities and goals, along with a robust governance and review process.

THE IMPACT

Transformational leaders genuinely add value. They are the glue that holds the organization together. They know their role and the potential of their position. They keep their eyes firmly on the organization's output and look to support others outside traditional confines.

Leaders know what their value system is. No matter the difficulty, they will not compromise their values, which include being truthful and having unquestionable integrity. They are mindful and self-aware, have excellent work-life management systems and take care of themselves. They are not focused on instant gratification or instant results. They are in it for the long haul and their decisions reflect this. Great leaders remain teachable and understand the value of introspection and feedback.

"The first issue that comes to mind is leaders who fail to actualize the importance of the role his or her team plays in actualizing the vision. I've seen great men and women, with great skills, great potential and great vision, who fail dismally in taking people along. In realizing that dream, I have come to learn that people and relationships matter for my role as a leader, and I see time and time again people missing the mark as far as that is concerned.

"The other issue is the inability to find the balance between work and home. I've seen many people get destroyed by failing to do that, so you end up not being as efficient, not being as effective as you can be as a leader because of that imbalance.

"Destroying your family life and hoping to succeed – I have seen from personal experience how that impacts one's ability and one's pursuit of whatever vision they are striving for at a point in time. So, I know from personal experience just how critical that is and how enriching it is to have a support structure like your family buying into your vision or buying into the dream you are working towards and actually making it possible for you to pursue that dream. You know that you have that strong base back home to support you."

Abey Kgotle
Executive Director, Human Resources, Mercedes-Benz
Johannesburg, South Africa

The impact of leading the business is as follows:

Past		Future	
Aloof	✗	Compassionate	✓
Bias	✗	Tolerance	✓
Denial	✗	Foresight	✓
Erratic	✗	Consistent	✓
Ignorant	✗	Truth	✓

SPENDING TIME
CRITICIZING THE PAST
ADDS NOTHING TO
MAKE THE FUTURE
A BETTER ONE.

LEADING THE INDUSTRY

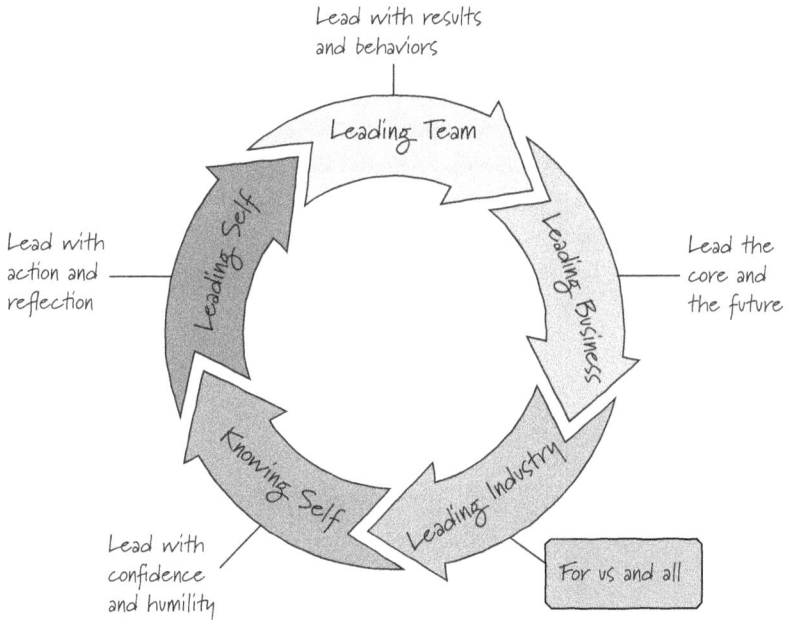

Lead with results
and behaviors

Leading Team

Leading Self

Lead with
action and
reflection

Leading Business

Lead the
core and
the future

Knowing Self

Leading Industry

Lead with
confidence
and humility

For us and all

PART 5

LEADING THE INDUSTRY: THE FUTURE BELONGS TO US AND IT IS FOR ALL

_____

Leading the industry encapsulates the concept of "for us (our company) and for all (the broader industry)". It is the contribution you could make to your business and the contribution you could make to the industry.

As you grow and develop as a business leader, you gain a deep understanding of your markets and products. This means you are in an ideal position to contribute to your industry. The industry you operate in plays an important role in setting the pace for government legislation, as well as for growth opportunities within the country. In other words, as a transformational leader, you have a say about the future of your company and the industry you operate in.

Leading the industry is not only about achieving sustainable self-leadership– it's about sharing best practices and establishing a vision for the industry. Are you in a position to influence the industry, stakeholders, governments and colleagues? It is an opportunity lost should you not help set the agenda.

STRATEGIC PERSPECTIVE: LEADING THE INDUSTRY

RELATIONSHIP MODEL SUPPORTING LEADING THE INDUSTRY

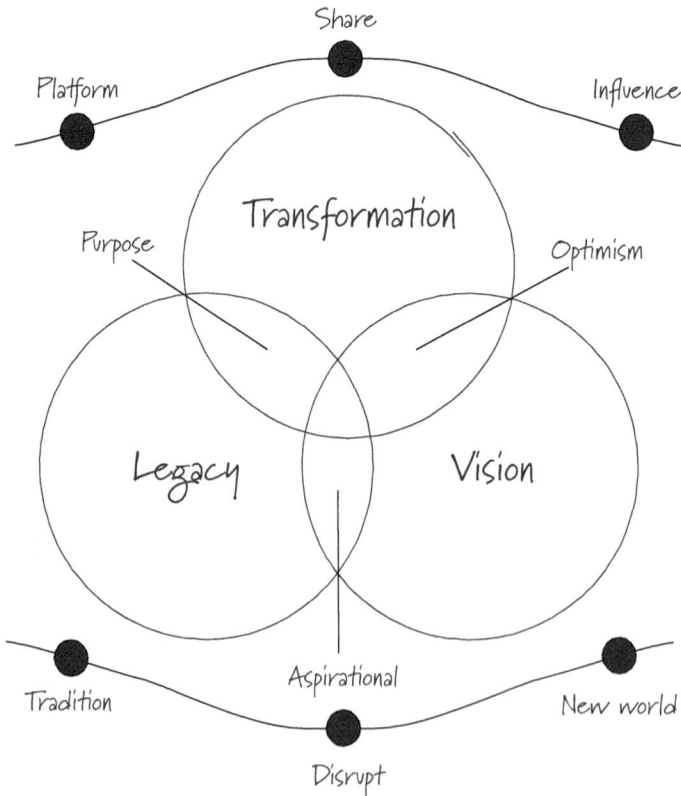

To gain a strategic perspective of leading the industry, let's look at the three core components.

1. TRANSFORMATION

To lead the industry is to cultivate transformational leadership. Transformational leadership takes place on three levels:

- **Self-transformation.** Parts 1 and 2 of this book deal with this idea in depth. Through the process of knowing the self and self-management, you can lead with confidence and humility on the one hand and action and reflection on the other.
- **Business transformation.** Transforming the business is about profitable growth. You sustain the core business in the present while simultaneously planning for the future. What are you doing to future-proof your business?
- **Industry transformation.** This is your contribution to changing and leading the way for your industry. It involves participating in and leading industry and government-related forums. These forums are where policy is discussed and industry impacts are determined. To truly transform the industry, you must also think about the broader society it serves.

"Your ability to reinvent yourself, to me, is a very important characteristic of leaders. And I say that from multiple dimensions. I think the first one is, you look at the way the world has changed even within the last 10, 15 years, and I'm not just talking about technology. Ten years back, five-year business plans were quite common. Today, most companies don't do that. I mean, they have a vision, but the world is moving so fast they just have to learn to adapt.

"But I think learning to adapt is a negative term. Leaders need to have vision, but they can only do that if they have reinvented themselves with a new technology, new management styles, working in a different way, remote working, working with technology. This ability to reinvent is so important.

"Otherwise, somebody like me born in the late '60s suddenly finds that the way they work has completely changed. Even what motivates people. What motivated people 10 years back is very different to what motivates people today. Management style, which was more command and control 15 to 20 years ago, has completely changed. The business environment has changed. Companies are getting more and more short term, faster. Look at Apple and how quickly they introduce new models of iPhones. Some of the biggest companies today don't own anything. Airbnb is the largest chain and they don't own a single hotel. Uber does not own a single car. So, the traditional things have all gone.

"Previously, you had to reinvent yourself every 10 years. I think you're going to do it now every two years or one year.

"The second thing is managing your time. I probably felt it when I moved from Ford to Nissan because of the scale of the job and scope. But, now looking at a lot of CEOs and senior people all over the world, they really have to learn how to manage their time, which includes having clarity of thought, being able to focus on the right stuff. There's always so much you can do and your list is always very long. You have to really be able to prioritize and manage your time.

"Last but not least, I still think in spite of all the changes, in spite of all the technology, leadership is becoming more relevant now than ever. Because in the past, your position as a leader was largely driven by your status in the organization. Today, it has to be far more earned than it was 10 or 15 years back. To me, leadership is going to be the real differentiating factor, even as technology gets more dominant in work and in the way we interact with each other. I think that personal interactions and leadership are becoming more critical.

"For me, these are the three things I see as a big shift compared to 15 years back. Fifteen years back, if you were a CEO, you got respect simply because you were a CEO. Today, that is not the case. Most leaders have to earn leadership status. People question leaders more. The shareholders question leaders more, the stock market questions leaders more. Leadership is more in demand now than ever before."

Kalyana Sivagnanam
President, Nissan Motor Corporation, and Regional Vice
President for Africa, Middle East and India
United Arab Emirates

2. LEGACY

What legacy do you want to leave? How do you want to be remembered? What impact do you want to make on the next generation? These are pertinent questions you must ask yourself when leading the industry.

Legacy happens on three levels:

- **Leaving a leadership legacy.** This is the ability to develop and nurture leaders. You must share your knowledge and experience and invest the time and effort into coaching and mentoring people. Encourage others to stretch themselves and step out of their comfort zones to develop and grow.
- **Creating a sustainable business.** How does your legacy impact the life of the business? Have you helped it develop the ability to cope with disruption? Strong leadership not only impacts short-term, quarter or even half-year results. It has far broader and long-lasting consequences for the business. It paves the way for the business's future.
- **Making the world a better place.** What have you done to change the world for the better? Has your leadership influenced and improved the lives of your employees, customers, broader society and environment? How active is your industry in reaching out to people who need your help and support?

LEAVING A LEGACY

How do I want to be remembered? We all ask this question at some point in our lives. What impression will we leave once we are gone? What will remain of us?

During my travels to a beautiful and desolate part of Southern Africa, I visited a place called Deadvlei, in the Namib-Naukluft Park in Namibia. "Deadvlei" means dead marsh and is the site of a white clay pan near the famous salt pan of Sossusvlei. It is reputed to be surrounded by the highest sand dunes in the world. On average, the dunes reach heights of between 300-400 meters.

According to the Namibia Tourism Board, the claypan formed more than 1,000 years ago when the Tsauchab River flooded after heavy rainfall and created shallow pools of water. Camel thorn trees grew in these marshes until the climate changed about 200 years later. Drought struck the area and the sand dunes encroached on the Tsauchab River, blocking any water from entering. The once luscious marshland soon disappeared.

With no water, the trees were unable to survive, but they did not disappear. So harsh was the climate, the trees dried out instead of decomposing. The desert sun scorched them into blackened bones. Now, these 900-year-old tree skeletons are trapped in the white clay, set against red-rusted dunes and a brilliant blue sky. A forest, frozen in time, a testament to times long past.

PART 5: LEADING THE INDUSTRY

What will be your legacy once you are gone? Do you inspire others and encourage them to achieve what they once believed impossible? Do you believe in others? Are you a good mentor and a wise coach? What example do you set? Are you kind and compassionate? Your legacy is not shaped at the end of your time – it is shaped every day by what you do and say. The relationships you create and the way you treat people are what you leave behind.

I believe a legacy is determined by:

- **Our value system** – what we stand for and what we would not compromise on in any situation.
- **Creativity and innovation** to test the status quo. What are we doing to make this a better, more sustainable world and place to work?
- **How we develop and guide** the people who are entrusted to our leadership.
- **How we make people feel** when they work with us.

In the words of author Maya Angelou, "If you're going to live, leave a legacy. Make a mark on the world that can't be erased."

3. VISION

To lead the industry, one must have clarity, insight and vision. There are three levels to this:

- **Clarity of purpose.** Do you have clarity regarding your intentions? What do you aspire to and what motivates you? What are you passionate about?
- **Clarity of performance.** What do you need to execute, accomplish and achieve?
- **Clarity of prospect.** What expectations do you have of yourself, your business and the industry? What is your outlook for the future?

"It sounds a little clichéd to say that you have to live a purpose-driven life or have a purpose-driven career, but maybe sharing some part of my personal life journey will be helpful.

"Getting into the financial advisory market was purely by accident. I had no pre-ordained plan that I was going to study and eventually become a financial adviser and end up in this industry. But when I found my footing in the industry, I realized this was something I thoroughly enjoyed because it involved making a difference to other people. My whole life, I've been taught by my mom that your core purpose in life as a human being is to change somebody else's life, to make a difference.

"You may not be able to change the world, but as long as you can leave the earth better than you found it, you would have lived your life's purpose. That resonated very strongly for me in becoming a corporate financial adviser because I was touching hundreds of thousands of these families and with many of them not knowing my name. This was their hard-earned money, their pension plans and their health plans and it was really about how do I make a difference to them?

"What was initially a purpose in my own life of breaking the cycle of poverty in my family has now gone on to the second generation of breaking the cycle of poverty. Now that we've achieved that quite successfully as a family, it's about breaking the cycle of poverty in the country.

"It's that purpose that really sort of gets you up and gets you out of bed in the morning and really makes you want to show up to work in a big way. We have massive rates of unemployment. We've got 54% of the country dependent on social grants, and 39% of South Africans, predominantly widows and orphans, are dependent on less than R980 a month. I ask myself, how do people actually live on this amount of money? It reminds me of my own upbringing. I look at these clients of mine and listen to the families that are really destitute, where employees are working in a manufacturing site or a mining site. I ask myself the question, what are we doing to make their lives better?

"I draw a lot of inspiration from Tony Robbins. There's no better thing than to actually give back. You'll never get a more rewarding feeling. And, in my opinion, I think the thing that really gets you out of bed in the morning and do the work is having some form of purpose that's bigger than you, more than just work. We feed over a 1,300 children daily every morning when they get to school. These kids are no different to me when I was a little boy."

Antony Govender
CEO, ASI Financial Services
South Africa

THE INTERSECTIONS

In the above model, the relationship between transformation, legacy and vision indicates a leader who is not only concerned with implementing templates and processes. They are the kind of leader who can deliver transformation. They have a sustainable vision for the future and can leave an enduring legacy. Their focus is firmly on how they can serve others, rather than what others can do for them. They inspire others through their sense of purpose and optimism.

At the three intersections are:

- **Purpose.** An unshakable belief in what you want to achieve. An unshakable belief requires the determination to succeed and a conviction for what you stand for.
- **Optimism.** Successful transformational leaders have a sense of optimism about the future and it is infectious. It inspires those around them to be brave. It brings calm to the organization because they create hope for a better future.
- **Aspirational.** People look up to these leaders. They aspire to walk in their shoes one day. These leaders have a can-do attitude, loads of ambition and dream big.

SUNSET ASSIGNMENTS

Experiencing elephants in the wild is a privilege and capturing them with a camera is always special.

On a recent trip to a game reserve, we came across a large, lone elephant bull. The bull was in "musth" – meaning he was primed to mate. As a result, he was aggressive and potentially dangerous. We stayed out of his way. As the tusker turned to amble away from us, the sun rose behind him, bathing him in a flood of golden light. We sat in silence as we observed this incredible sight.

I often hear of long-serving employees embarking on "sunset assignments". This refers to one's last assignment or position before entering retirement. I am not a fan of this term, as it sounds like the end is near and it is a fast track downhill from there!

Most of our working life is spent focused on our careers, during which we gain insights from life's many lessons. As we get older, we become wiser and should find ways to apply our knowledge for the benefit of others as well as ourselves. Look for ways to do this by:

- **Putting your experiences to good use.** People at this point in their lives have gained a range of experiences – some good, some bad. Take what you have learned and put it to good use. Follow your passion. You are more than qualified and have all the experience you will ever need.

- **Giving back.** Now is the time to give back – to yourself, to your community and to the younger generation. Mentorship and coaching are rewarding ways to develop, encourage and teach others.
- **Staying active.** Keep the body, mind and soul busy. Read, learn and find new things to study and think about. Keeping physically active provides energy and longevity and does wonders for a general sense of well-being.

Just as the old elephant bull walked off into the sunset, new horizons are waiting for you. There are new places to visit and new experiences to be had. Your "sunset assignment" is really your next "sunrise assignment"! Look at this time in your life as a new beginning rather than the end of a chapter. Set yourself on a path of opportunity and rewarding work. You will never regret this.

After all, this evening's sunset is tomorrow's sunrise!

CULTIVATING INDUSTRY LEADERSHIP IN A DISRUPTIVE WORLD

As previously discussed, disruption is no longer a catchphrase; it is a business reality. For leaders, disruption typically takes place on two levels:

- Long-standing business models are disrupted.
- The self is disrupted. To effectively deal with business disruption, leaders must take a good look at themselves. How you respond to disruption can either propel or derail you. What would propel you forward in this uncertain environment?

According to KPMG's Global CEO Outlook 2017[1], disruption and growth are inseparable. Constant change, even in uncertain times, is increasingly necessary for businesses to succeed. In fact, KPMG Australia CEO Gary Wingrove says CEOs are required to be the disruptors. They must challenge their own roles and business models to lead their companies and industries to success.

As we look to the future, what will be the key disruptors globally?

- **Customer base.** This is likely to continue to be the biggest driver of global disruption. How customers want their products, in what form, where and when will continue to disrupt any business model, impacting distribution channels and methodologies.
- **Technological advances.** Better and smarter technology requires more efficient production processes.

---

1 "Global CEO Outlook 2017: The Outlook for Australia," KPMG, 2017. https://home.kpmg.com/au/en/home/insights/2017/06/global-ceo-outlook-2017-australia.html

*   **Competitors.** Emerging competitors in sectors previously protected by patents and high entry costs are adding to the rapid rate of disruption.

We cannot prevent disruption. It will continue whether we like it or not. The key for you as a leader is to prepare yourself and your industry for it.

WHAT BUSINESS TRENDS CAN WE EXPECT IN THE FUTURE?

Dealing with disruption means identifying and working with trends. *Forbes* has identified the top 10 business trends for 2018 and beyond[2], which will impact leaders and organizations of all sizes. Some of these include:

*   **Artificial intelligence.** AI drives customer experience. Innovative leaders realize that using AI to perform repeatable and redundant tasks does not eliminate human interaction, it enriches it.
*   **Communities embrace live interactions over social media.** Top companies realize building greater communities engenders brand loyalty. Nothing drives strong communities better than in-person and live interactions.
*   **Social learning outperforms remote learning.** Social learning takes place through peer social interaction. Successful companies must develop mentoring and coaching tools that leverage internal expertise organically.

---

2 Ian Altman, "The Top 10 Business Trends That Will Drive Success In 2018," *Forbes*, December 5, 2017. https://www.forbes.com/sites/ianaltman/2017/12/05/the-top-business-trends-that-will-drive-success-in-2018/#351e2f23701a

- **Live streaming video content gains momentum.** Customers demand real connections with real people. Companies that plan for and dedicate resources to produce live-stream videos will dominate their industries.
- **Millennials welcome Generation Z.** Gen Zs (those born after 1998) are entering their formative years and their influence is increasing. It is estimated this group will soon outnumber their Millennial predecessors. Millennials are increasingly in leadership positions and will soon supervise Gen Z employees. Will the Millennials complain as much about Gen Z employees as the Baby Boomers did of Millennials? Gen Z consumers are the first generation born with devices in their hands, so smart leaders are racing to understand the impact of Gen Z both as consumers and as employees.

As you can see, cultivating leadership for this unpredictable environment is essential for leaders, businesses and industries to survive. Rather than perceiving it as negative, leaders must view this environment as a world of opportunities waiting to be leveraged.

To cultivate disruptive leadership, consider the following strategies:

- **Challenge your leadership and role.** Is your role one of positional power or do you empower and influence your team to innovate, take risks and be creative?
- **Self-development.** Senior executives are spending more time than ever on self-development and self-management strategies. As this book has demonstrated, there are enormous benefits to understanding what drives you and what derails you as a leader.

- **Two-way focus.** Focus on leveraging your core business, but remember to develop strategies to enter future growth businesses.
- **Build organizational resilience.** A disruptive environment has a significant impact on employee well-being and their ability to manage their work and personal lives. You must equip your workers with the tools to cope. As Steve Worrall, managing director of Microsoft Australia, says: "New technology is exacerbating people's already demanding lives. So, empathy is critical for senior leaders to enable their employees to be more efficient and productive. I want to ensure my team and my clients are not overwhelmed. They need to have a sense of well-being and balance to thrive in the complex environment, but also to have a rich and full life with their families."
- **Focus and exploit cognitive technology.** Cognitive technology – such as robotics, speech recognition and machine learning – will most certainly impact headcount levels, but smarter, more technological ways of doing business can also open avenues for job creation.

Working with disruption and viewing it as an opportunity rather than a threat builds leadership agility and future-proofs leaders, their businesses and their industries.

AI IS THE NEW FRONTIER IN BUSINESS

The fascinating documentary *Do You Trust This Computer?* made its world premiere on April 5, 2018. It examines the staggering amount of data collected, interpreted and fed back to us through apps, intelligent devices and targeted ads.

The film explores the rise of data analytics and machine learning and its power to fundamentally transform society – from influencing elections (Cambridge Analytica) to medical diagnostics and even battlefield weapons. Director Chris Paine said the impetus for the film was to explore "how AI has started to redefine our relationship with computers. How fast is this tech accelerating? What does it promise us? Are there truly 'existential threats'? And perhaps the biggest question, can we control what we've created?"[3]

If AI is the new frontier in business, what does AI, machine learning and robotics mean for leaders, companies and industries? How will leaders react? What are their roles and responsibilities? How will employees react?

EMPLOYEE REACTIONS

In April 2018, approximately 3,100 Google employees, including senior-level engineers, sent a protest letter to Google CEO Sundar Pichai, demanding the company pull out of a controversial AI project called "Project Maven". The petition said the project flew in the face of the company's "don't be evil" mantra. In May, about a dozen Google employees resigned in protest of the company's involvement.[4]

The project involved Google assisting the Pentagon to improve the US military's use of drone strikes. The aim was to speed up analysis of drone footage by using AI to classify images of objects and people automatically.

---

3 Chris Paine, "Do You Trust This Computer?" LinkedIn, April 5, 2018. https://www.linkedin.com/pulse/do-you-trust-computer-chris-paine/

4 Scott Shane and Daisuke Wakabayashi, "'The Business of War': Google Employees Protest Work for the Pentagon," *The New York Times*, April 4, 2018. https://www.nytimes.com/2018/04/04/technology/google-letter-ceo-pentagon-project.html

However, in June 2018, an email was sent to Google employees to inform them that the company wouldn't renew the contract with Project Maven. Furthermore, Google cloud chief Diane Greene said the company would not pursue further Department of Defense contracts.

CUSTOMER REACTIONS

In April 2018, a California judge ruled that Facebook must face a class action lawsuit over its use of facial recognition technology. The lawsuit alleged Facebook had gathered users' biometric information without their explicit consent. This involved the "tag suggestions" technology, which spots users' friends in uploaded photos. The lawsuit said this breached Illinois state law.[5]

In his order, US District Judge James Donato said Facebook seemed to believe individual lawsuits would be preferable to a class action "because statutory damages could amount to billions of dollars".

SOCIETY REACTIONS

In 2017, Tesla and SpaceX chief executive Elon Musk renewed calls for the proactive regulation of AI because "by the time we are reactive in AI regulation, it's too late".[6]

Musk said: "Normally the way regulations are set up is when a bunch of bad things happen, there's a public outcry, and after

---

5 "Facebook facial recognition faces class-action suit," BBC News, April 17, 2018. https://www.bbc.com/news/technology-43792125

6 Samuel Gibbs, "Elon Musk: regulate AI to combat 'existential threat' before it's too late," *The Guardian*, July 17, 2017. https://www.theguardian.com/technology/2017/jul/17/elon-musk-regulation-ai-combat-existential-threat-tesla-spacex-ceo

many years a regulatory agency is set up to regulate that industry. It takes forever. That, in the past, has been bad but not something which represented a fundamental risk to the existence of civilisation.

"AI is the rare case where I think we need to be proactive in regulation instead of reactive. Because I think by the time we are reactive in AI regulation, it'll be too late."

"Again, I'm going to come back to the earlier conversation by saying this is an integration we have never seen before. Now, Elon Musk is talking about artificial intelligence on Mars, but it's not going to be restricted to the vehicles that he is putting in space. It is going to come into the workforce whether you're manufacturing baby diapers or whether you are manufacturing rockets.

"The second issue is ethics, which is probably going to be a bigger issue. Again, it's going to make demands on leadership as previously we could clearly define what ethics were. We could define what is technology and we could define what is your product. I think very soon, these three things are going to merge. I'll give you a small example and I think this is the debate that Google is now having with drones.

"Do you know what is stopping the real development of autonomous cars? There are three things. First is technology. Technology is already there. Today, there are cars that can drive autonomously. That's not an issue. The second thing is legislation. Things like who pays if there's an accident – is it the car maker, is it some kind of platform that monitors these cars? Because if you look at the aviation industry, there are planes flying in the air, but there's an air traffic control that monitors all this. Tomorrow, if there are thousands of autonomous cars, they have to be monitored, they have to be managed by some kind of platform. That platform doesn't exist, so it's not the autonomous car technology that doesn't exist, it's the platform that manages it. The other complication is in the air, you don't have some manual and some autonomous planes, but on the ground you are going to have, for some time, some vehicles that are autonomous and some vehicles that will be driven by bad drivers. So, we still don't have the technology that has the platform that can manage this, but even all this is not the real issue.

"The real issue that people are grappling with is the issue of ethics. For example, a car is driving on Sheikh Zayed Road at 120km per hour and there is an old man who is crossing the road and the crash is inevitable. Do you program the car to save the occupant or do you program the car to save the pedestrian? Who makes the decision? What if there was a child on the road? Would the child have a preference over adults sitting in the car? What if you have 10 adults in the car and one small child on the road? Would you sacrifice 10 adults to save the child? What if there is a child on the road and a child in the car? What does the vehicle software do?

"So, the real issue is that all these things are now merging: technology, ethics, societal values and product. Previously, they were so clearly separated that it was very easy for you to make these decisions without them having an impact on each other. Privacy, your ethics, your technology and your product are all merging. Convergence and how to handle this is the big question leaders of the future will grapple with."

Kalyana Sivagnanam
President, Nissan Motor Corporation, and Regional Vice
President for Africa, Middle East and India
United Arab Emirates

LEADERSHIP RESPONSIBILITY

Society is becoming increasingly aware of the AI "threat". It is affecting employees (as seen in the Google example) and customers (as in the Facebook case). AI has become part of our business reality and leaders must take an active role in understanding its benefits and potential hazards.

Key findings in the 2017 PwC Global CEO Report explain the impact of robotics and AI and how CEOs should respond: "Twenty years ago, there were fewer than 700,00 industrial robots worldwide; today there are 1.8 million, and the number is expected to soar to 2.6 million in another two years. More than three-quarters of CEOs globally believe technology will cause job losses over the next five years. The role of the CEO is not to see this as a threat, but to recognize the window of opportunity to rethink and redesign the way they employ, manage and interact with people."[7]

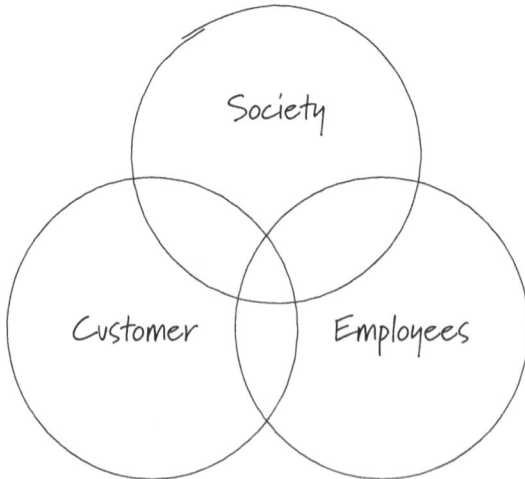

7 "It's the end of HR as we know it," PwC, 2017. https://www.pwc.com.au/ceo-agenda/ceo-survey/2017/key-findings/talent.html

INVESTMENT IN AI IS GROWING

Leaders cannot ignore the fact that investment in AI, robotics and cognitive technology is growing. In the US, artificial intelligence funding peaked in Q3'18 and AI-related companies raised $9.3 billion full-year in 2018. This represents a staggering 72% increase compared to 2017![8]

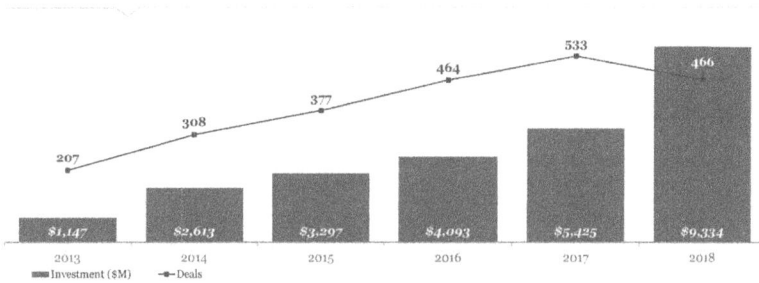

AI: US annual funding

AI-related funding jumps sharply after increasing every year since 2013

- AI-related companies raised $9.3B in 2018, a 72% increase compared to 2017.
- Deal activity dipped to 466 from 533 in 2017, after increasing for four years.

Investment ($M): $1,147 (2013), $2,613 (2014), $3,297 (2015), $4,093 (2016), $5,425 (2017), $9,334 (2018)

Deals: 207 (2013), 308 (2014), 377 (2015), 464 (2016), 533 (2017), 466 (2018)

The flow of money into AI startups comes as sophisticated computing technologies, such as machine learnings, speech recognition and image recognition, have graduated from the labs and made their way into the commercial market.

8 PwC/CB Insights, "MoneyTree Report: Q4 2018", https://www.pwc.com/us/en/moneytree-report/moneytree-report-q4-2018.pdf.

THE IMPACT OF AI ON LEADERSHIP

Not even leadership itself will be spared from the impact of AI. In fact, it is predicted that AI will supplant many aspects of the "hard" elements of leadership, the parts responsible for the raw cognitive processing of facts and information.

Furthermore, it is predicted that AI will lead to greater emphasis and need for the "soft" elements of leadership — the personality traits, attitudes and behaviors required for individuals to help others achieve a common goal.[9]

It is easy for leaders to feel threatened by AI, robotics and machine learning. However, AI cannot emulate the soft elements of leadership. This is where the responsibility of leadership lies.

---

9 Tomas Chamorro-Premuzic, Michael Wade and Jennifer Jordan, "As AI Makes More Decisions, the Nature of Leadership Will Change," *Harvard Business Review*, January 22, 2018. https://hbr.org/2018/01/as-ai-makes-more-decisions-the-nature-of-leadership-will-change#)

"As for the internet, there might be some disadvantages, but there are also compelling arguments as to how positively it's changed our lives. There are some forms of AI where you can mimic certain aspects of being human and human behavior and that will introduce efficiencies into a system, but you can't mimic other aspects of human behavior that are present in a human and override potential unethical or immoral dangers inside the process.

"I'll give you an example. AI is used in a lot of call centers now. But what if the call center is embedded in the government department, in a social services area, and looking after aged people in the society? The elderly person rings up and says, 'I'm a pensioner,' and they're asked their name and address and so on so they're identified, and then they say, 'I can't pay my electricity bill this quarter and I understand there's a system within the government to get some assistance with my bill because I'm a pensioner.'

"The automated response checks everything in an instant and says, 'Yes, you are correct. However, the rule is that you can only access that relief once a year and six months ago, in the first quarter, you already drew down on that. Unfortunately, we cannot help you.'

"The person responds by saying, 'Yes, I am aware of that rule. However, my husband has become very, very ill, and we're coming into winter now and we're going to have our heating and lighting cut off. Will I be able to cook? Will I be able to see after 5pm at night? Will it be freezing?'

"And the rules simply say you can only access it once a year. The artificial intelligence can only regurgitate the rules that are being fed into it and the history of that particular client.

"It will be likely to deny that request, whereas a human being would say, 'Yes, you're asking for a violation of the rule. However, there are extreme extenuating circumstances here,' and if they don't have the authority to overrule the rule, they will escalate it to a superior. At the moment, there are limitations with AI, I believe, around moral and ethical thinking. Until AI can catch up with that element of the human brain, I think we're in a period of risk."

Dr David Cooke
Chairman and Managing Director, Konica Minolta Australia
Adjunct Professor, UTS Business School, Sydney, Australia

IQ AND EQ

AI is not only changing the way we do business. It's changing the way we lead.

In a *Harvard Business Review* article, authors Megan Beck and Barry Libert make the point that we've already accepted that automated systems can do tasks such as data gathering and analysis efficiently. "A human being, however, is still best suited to jobs like spurring the leadership team to action, avoiding political hot buttons, and identifying savvy individuals to lead change."[10]

Consulting firm McKinsey & Company has been studying the areas in which machines are best suited to replace humans. What kind of work is most adaptable to automation? Their findings suggest technical and tactical as opposed to strategic thinking. This is because work that requires a high degree of imagination, creative analysis and strategic thinking is more difficult to program.

According to McKinsey: "The hardest activities to automate with currently available technologies are those that involve managing and developing people (9% automation potential) or that apply expertise to decision making, planning or creative work (18%)."[11]

Computers are great at optimizing, but not so great at goal-setting or using common sense. This means leaders must leverage their human capabilities to differentiate themselves in the future.

10 Megan Beck and Barry Libert, "The Rise of AI Makes Emotional Intelligence More Important," *Harvard Business Review*, February 15, 2017. https://hbr.org/2017/02/the-rise-of-ai-makes-emotional-intelligence-more-important

11 Michael Chui, James Manyika and Mehdi Miremadi, "Where machines could replace humans – and where they can't (yet)," *McKinsey Quarterly*, July 2016. https://www.mckinsey.com/business-functions/digital-mckinsey/our-insights/where-machines-could-replace-humans-and-where-they-cant-yet

PART 5: LEADING THE INDUSTRY

Indeed, 50 years of research suggests that personality traits, such as curiosity and emotional stability (EQ), are twice as important as IQ – the benchmark for reasoning capability – when it comes to leadership effectiveness.[12]

As AI gains momentum, we need to re-think the essence of effective leadership. Domain experience and authority are becoming less important. Engagement, humility, creativity, initiative, adaptability and vision will play key roles in morale-boosting and industry-building leadership.

How are you and your company preparing future leaders for this? How are you preparing yourself and your industry for this change in leadership style?

---

12 Tomas Chamorro-Premuzic, Michael Wade and Jennifer Jordan, "As AI Makes More Decisions, the Nature of Leadership Will Change," *Harvard Business Review*, January 22, 2018. https://hbr.org/2018/01/as-ai-makes-more-decisions-the-nature-of-leadership-will-change#)

"We talk about the future of work and how things are changing with the introduction and the evolution of artificial intelligence and robotics and analytics. Companies need to understand how they can maximize data and analytics and then upskill their people to make use of that data to take it to another level.

"In many organizations, a lot of our time is spent on number crunching and data and doing spreadsheets and the Excel files, but whether it is due to skill or time constraints, we often do not leverage this data. Organizations that can maximize and upskill their people in the digital age and can leverage new innovative thinking will see a value to the business. I don't see robotics and artificial learning as something to fear. I see it as an opportunity for people to have more rewarding work, to add real value to the company and directly impact the bottom line with real change.

"From a company perspective, it is an exciting time of change. However, how we manage our communication with employees, how we develop them, how we leverage these challenges will be critical in determining whether the transition will be a successful or a difficult one."

Gayle Antony
General Manager, Head of Global Learning and Development,
Nissan Motor Company
Nashville, United States

FOLLOW-THROUGH: THE ROADMAP TO LEADING THE INDUSTRY

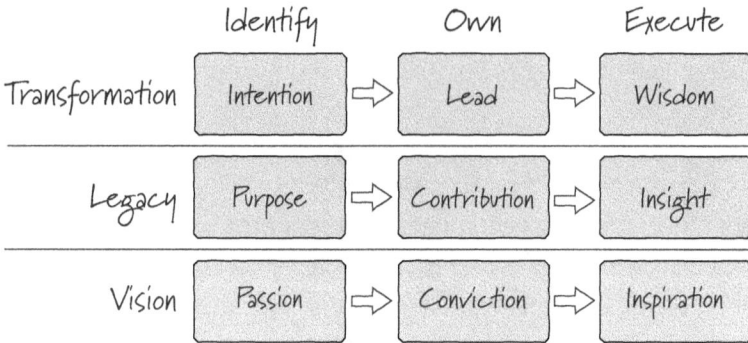

	Identify		Own		Execute
Transformation	Intention	⇨	Lead	⇨	Wisdom
Legacy	Purpose	⇨	Contribution	⇨	Insight
Vision	Passion	⇨	Conviction	⇨	Inspiration

Execution is putting the tactical components of leadership for the industry to work. The roadmap to successful execution is through a process of **identification**, **ownership** and **delivery (execution)** of nine leading the industry components:

TRANSFORMATION

1. IDENTIFY INTENTION

What are your intentions? What do you want to achieve? Leadership at this level can be lonely. It takes a certain amount of skill to survive. Be clear about your intentions for yourself, your business and the industry. Ask yourself the following:

- Do I have the **determination** to see it through it? Do I have a resolute plan with a purposeful approach?
- Do I have the **commitment** to do this? Leadership at this level is a call to action that involves dealing with the consequences.
- Do I have the **resolve** to see it through?

COMMITMENT

The Karl Theodor Bridge, also known as the Old Bridge or "Alte Brücke", is a stone bridge over the Neckar River in Heidelberg, Germany. It connects the Old City with the eastern part of the Neuenheim district on the opposite bank. The bridge was built in 1788, constructed from Neckar Valley sandstone. It is one of the best-known landmarks in Heidelberg, reputed to be one of the most romantic cities in Germany.

It is not surprising, then, that Alte Brücke is also the site of hundreds of love locks. Lovers pledge their endless love and commitment to one another by attaching a lock to the metal girders of the bridge.

Commitment indicates sincere and unchanging purpose. It is the act of binding and engaging oneself emotionally and intellectually to a course of action.

Committed people are people of action. They get things done. Committed leaders keep going in the face of adversity. They accept the obligation to do something and remain dedicated to a cause or activity. They are willing to give time and energy to something they firmly believe in.

What makes a committed leader? What characteristics do they possess?

- **Call to action.** A committed leader accepts the call to action, along with all its consequences.

- **Your word is your bond.** A committed leader's word is sacrosanct. Regardless of adversity and challenges, they always keep their word.
- **Consistency.** A committed leader would make the same decision given the same set of circumstances. They never make a decision based on what others want to hear or see.

In his book, *Long Walk to Freedom*, Nelson Mandela said: "I had no epiphany, no singular revelation, no moment of truth, but a steady accumulation of a thousand slights, a thousand indignities and a thousand unremembered moments produced in me an anger, a rebelliousness, a desire to fight the system that imprisoned my people. There was no particular day on which I said, henceforth I will devote myself to the liberation of my people; instead, I simply found myself doing so, and could not do otherwise."

Great leaders answer the call to action. Their commitment to what they believe in is always at the forefront of their minds, motivating their actions. Commitment is an essential element of any leadership success story.

2. OWN YOUR LEADERSHIP

This is the ability to inspire. Leading at this level involves leading yourself and being a beacon for your business and your industry. You bring out the best in others.

As Matt Church, founder of Thought Leaders, says: "In essence, leadership is about bringing out greatness in the people around you. I think leadership is about this idea more than about vision, or strategy, or planning. Fix your attention on this one thing as a leader, and you end up with a superpower of sorts; the leadership capability to inspire and not simply inform."[13]

3. EXECUTE WISDOM

Take the experiences and knowledge you've gained over the years and apply them in such a way that they benefit and are of value to those you lead. Wisdom is about applying common sense and good judgment.

LEGACY

4. IDENTIFY YOUR PURPOSE

When you do something with purpose, you do it with determination and conviction. Identifying your purpose provides you with a sense of direction. This creates meaning for you and those around you as you strive to achieve your goals. As success coach and author Jack Canfield says, "Identifying, acknowledging, and honouring this purpose is perhaps the most important action successful people

13 Matt Church, "Above the Line," LinkedIn Pulse, December 19, 2017. https://www.linkedin.com/pulse/above-line-matt-church/

take. They take the time to understand what they're here to do –
and then they pursue that with passion and enthusiasm."[14]

5. OWN YOUR CONTRIBUTION

Your legacy is defined in terms of what you have contributed
to your business, your industry and society. A contribution is a
gift – a gift of yourself, your energy and your time. What can you
contribute?

- **To society.** How have you and your industry contributed to
  improving society?
- **To your employees.** Are you a role model for your employees?
  Do you develop them? This should be one of your key focus
  areas – to nurture, grow and develop those you lead.
- **To your customers.** Do you form long-lasting and trusting
  relationships with your customers through a strong brand? A
  great contribution involves the ability to create trust in your
  product, your brand and within the industry.

---

14 Jack Canfield, "How to Identify and Honor Your Life Purpose." http://jackcanfield.com/
blog/are-you-living-your-passion/

"I was in a small executive leadership session a few years ago, and the chairman of the (global) company came in. It was just after the previous CEO had stepped out and a new CEO was in the role. He (the chairman) must have been in an introspective mood, because one of the first things he said was, 'There's nothing sadder than an ex-CEO.' He started to talk about calls he had and, of course, he, himself, is an ex-CEO.

"He was describing how your entire life is built around this idea that 'all of my power and influence and what I think is important', and suddenly it's gone. So, suddenly either I retire or I'm pushed out. He said, 'I've watched these people who had all the power and money in the world, and the next month, their phone isn't ringing, they're not important. All of those things that were reaffirming to them or validating their existence are gone.'

"His advice to this group of senior execs was, 'Make sure that your life has purpose beyond work.' I thought it was really an astute, fairly profound piece of advice, coming from someone who knows. And, of course, he's financially secure, so maybe it's unfair to take advice from a billionaire, but I thought it was profound. Just this idea that your life needs to have meaning. You need to have respect. All these questions around, 'If you died tomorrow, who would show up at your funeral and why would they be there?'"

David Everhart
Senior Vice President, Leaders and Talents, Mannaz A/S
London, United Kingdom

PART 5: LEADING THE INDUSTRY

6. EXECUTE INSIGHT

What will leadership look like 15 years from now? Have you thought about the kind of leadership needed in the future?

Recently, Microsoft CEO Satya Nadella interviewed Carlos Ghosn, CEO of the Renault-Nissan-Mitsubishi Alliance, who spoke about the leadership of the future: "The challenge we are facing is that we know what type of leadership attributes we need for today. We do not know what attributes we need for the leader of tomorrow, 10 or 15 years from now, because so much transformation in the industry, technology, society is happening, and we are not sure exactly what we need or what we're going to need, so we can't be sure of our requirements. We can't be safe in our current choices even as we have them today."

Although we may not know exactly what the future holds for leadership, we do know it will be necessary for leaders to undergo a major transformational process to be successful. What insights do you have about your leadership in the future of your industry?

"The way I look at it is what does the function of work look like in the future? And how will organizations be structured? This talks to the second principle I believe in, which is what is the purpose of the businesses? Not its vision statement or charter, but what actually does the business stand for and how will it make a difference in the future?

"The nature of work is fundamentally changing. To be a leader in a future business, going into an office, sitting at a cubicle desk or corner office, whatever, is archaic.

"The amount of people I see working from coffee shops, telecommuting, co-working spaces, etc., and, more importantly, working for multiple organisations is how the future of work will look. For example, when I built a platform for a global classified business, I did not physically meet my team, yet we were able to effectively deliver the project within the timeframe and KPIs. My team was dispersed, my lead architect was based in San Francisco, my financial team in Amsterdam, my legal team was based in Sydney and my development team was based in Vietnam. Now, what's interesting here is what role does the company and its culture play in a dispersed organization of this nature? Why would a bunch of geographically dispersed freelancers work this way? For me, the common bond and focus comes down to, 'What is your business purpose?'

"Virgin is one of the first businesses I've worked for that truly embraces being a purpose-led organization. We look, develop and test our purpose against all the pillars of our business from a consumer, business partner, staff member and societal perspective. For me, it is critical to give back to the ecosystem that you created or are part of.

"If a leader has that philosophy, then the role of AI, drone technology, etc. should all be managed within that framework, and if the purpose is strong enough, everybody benefits in that network without anybody being worse off. If you can achieve that, then I think that's a true future leadership position to take."

Andre Hugo
CEO, Virgin Money
South Africa

VISION

7. IDENTIFY YOUR PASSION

The best way to achieve a sense of fulfilment and accomplishment is to identify and follow your passion. People say that when they follow their passion, "work" is no longer work because they love every minute of what they do. It is much easier to remain enthusiastic, inspired and motivated when you follow your passion. Passion helps you face your fears and take a leap of faith. Passionate leaders are the ones who push boundaries and take their industry forward.

"The best leaders are the ones who are absolutely passionate about the business. These are leaders who are genuinely passionate about what they are doing and the business they are in. They are totally invested in the opportunities the business gives them and those around them.

"This level of passion is very difficult if not impossible to fake. There is a gulf between leaders who are faking it and leaders who are passionate. Passionate leaders are the ones who are looking for every possible opportunity to develop themselves and the business and to grow employees. They fully immerse themselves in what they do.

"The other thing that really makes a difference from a leadership perspective is when leaders understand they are having an effect on the ecosystem, but that they are not the ecosystem. They get their results through other people so they can create some of the system, but they need other people to get in there and populate it (the ecosystem) and grow it. They're the people who realize they can only be great and business can only be great if you get the right people, and that takes time. It takes a lot of work. It's committing yourself to getting those people. That is why I will wake up in the mornings and get excited about working every day. There are other leaders who aren't particularly excited about the business. They don't have a genuine passion for what they do. They do it because it earns money or gives them power."

Daryl Mahon
Vice President HR, Ford
Australia and New Zealand

8. OWN CONVICTION

This is the knowledge that what you believe is true. It is also about knowing what needs to change. Conviction manifests in three ways:

- **Certainty.** It's that confidence you have within yourself. You know that what you are doing is right for your industry, your business and your customers.
- **Belief.** You back yourself and know your solutions are the best ones.
- **Resolution.** You are the beacon that guides the way. Even when times are challenging, difficult, disruptive and turbulent, be the one to light the way for others.

"It is about ultra-confidence and gravitas. That's the one key thing that sticks out from all the senior people I've worked with who had a massive impact on organizations.

"However, this confidence can create blind spots for them, too. It might derail them personally or produce extra risk in the organization because they're not paying attention to some of the noise that's coming up. I think that can be a problem with the powerful leaders in that they're used to listening to people with big voices and, sometimes, you've got to listen to the smaller voices, especially when it's within risk and compliance, the control functions, and such like. You've got to pay attention to those details.

"But, ultimately, one of the other factors that most senior leaders have that springs to mind is intelligence. A lot of them ruffle feathers because they have ultra-confidence. They're powering through. They're knocking walls and they have a laser focus on what they want to deliver, which is what you need to have a great chief executive."

Aaron Clayton
Human Resources Director
United Arab Emirates

PART 5: LEADING THE INDUSTRY

9. EXECUTE INSPIRATION

A transformational leader inspires people to believe they can achieve whatever they set out to achieve. Traditional leadership is relatively isolated because it focuses on power and position. Over time, this can cause the business to stagnate and contract.

The leadership of the future, on the other hand, is collaborative. It will inspire the workforce, engage teams and encourage creativity and innovation. It is all about the expansion of the self, the business and the industry. Ultimately, this is how businesses and industries will survive the age of disruption.

"There's absolutely no doubt, and I see it in our business, you've got this new generation of people coming through that want to talk to the CEO. They're not interested in going via the channels. They want to talk to the CEO, they want to bounce their ideas off the CEO. You can't stop that. You've got to try to manage it in a way where it doesn't upset their immediate superior. So, you try to have this very open sort of channel of communication in your business. What they want out of a work environment is completely different to what the Baby Boomers and the next generation after that want.

"It's less about security; it's more about the ability to come up with new ideas and challenge the way it's always been done. To be able to talk directly to the CEO, they don't want us to follow these corporate channels."

Gary Neubert
CEO, EIE Group, Johannesburg, South Africa

THE IMPACT

Cultivating leadership for our unpredictable environment is not only required, it is essential for survival. But rather than see disruption as negative, leaders should view it as an opportunity to be embraced.

In this disruptive age, we need to re-assess what effective leadership is. What are the key ingredients that motivate, inspire and engage our workforce? The new face of leadership is one of organic and transformational growth. It moves leaders away from positions of power to positions of influence. The future of business requires the emergence of disruptive leaders who thrive and grow in the face of disruption.

"How do you enable creativity at the junior levels of an organization? While the world is changing, requiring more creativity and innovation, the need to have strong foundations and technical competence remains. You don't have to be an expert in every discipline, but you do need to have enough skills to be able to sort good ideas from bad ideas.

"To explain this in terms of a metaphor, I have this picture in my head that creativity in organizations is evolving from a marching band to a jazz band. In a marching band, everyone marches in step with the drum major, who is the leader and has control. Each instrument has their particular, clearly defined role to play, and the parts come together to create the desired sound.

"As the pace of environmental change accelerates, organizations need to become more like jazz bands. In jazz, musicians have a role to play within a framework. The drummer provides the beat that keeps the group together; however, there is also the space to ad lib. Musicians are expected to improvise, embellish and push the boundaries. Sometimes it will sound great and sometimes it won't – but you have created a culture where experimentation is OK and part of the journey.

"When we tie this back to the question of creativity and innovation, most musicians would argue that you need good, solid technical skills before moving on to live improvisation. Years of practising scales and chords sit behind every seemingly effortless and groovy jazz solo. Ad-libbing looks sexy, but it only sounds good if you have the skills to pull it off. So it is in our organizations! Creativity and innovation need to be built on strong foundations."

Kirsty Appleton
General Manager, Human Resources
Australia

"I think, definitely, with the elimination of expertise and moving into AI, it highlights the need to move from authority to influence even further. It really highlights that need. If anything, IQ should no longer be about intelligence. IQ should be about the ability to inspire, to influence. That's what IQ should change to.

"In this day and age, yes, I think leaders have to have great IQs, but I need influence ability. I need inspirational ability. It's not intellectual. Intellectualism has been commodified. You can get intellectual from Google within seconds. Intellectualism is not where it's at. Can you inspire and influence? That's the test of great leadership."

Kris Kumfert
Chief Human Resources Officer, Clark Pacific
United States

The impact of leading the industry is as follows:

Old world	New world
Ignorance ✗	Compassionate ✓
Power ✗	Influence ✓
Indifference ✗	Innovative ✓
Stagnate ✗	Disrupt ✓
Isolated ✗	Open ✓

GREAT LEADERS ANSWER THE CALL TO ACTION. THEIR COMMITMENT TO WHAT THEY BELIEVE TO BE TRUE AND OF VALUE IS ALWAYS AT THE FOREFRONT OF THEIR MINDS. COMMITMENT, RESOLVE AND DETERMINATION REMAIN ESSENTIAL ELEMENTS IN ANY SUCCESS STORY.

PART 6

THE FUTURE OF LEADERSHIP

As we have explored, machine learning and artificial intelligence will have a profound effect on the future of markets, industries and workforces.

Smart machines may be able to diagnose complex business problems and recommend actions to improve an organization. This means human capabilities, such as curiosity, innovation and creativity, will become increasingly valued over the next decade. Skills such as persuasion, social understanding and empathy will be the differentiators as AI takes over tactical tasks. It is critical your leadership encompasses these critical human skills and capabilities.

INSPIRATIONAL LEADERSHIP MODEL

Leadership	Impact	% Engagement
Influential	Exponential	80+
Impactful	Expanding	60
Progressive	Stable	40
Traditional	Stagnate	20
Isolated	Contract	10

"I'm a firm believer that irrespective of how much technology there is, people will always do business with people. I'm a firm believer that you've got to use technology to make your businesses more effective and efficient, but at the end of the day, people do business with people."

Gary Neubert
CEO, EIE Group
Johannesburg, South Africa

The leadership of the future will shift on three levels:

1. FROM TACTICAL TO INSPIRATIONAL

Cognitive technology, robotic-process automation and AI will implement the tactical elements of leadership. In the age of disruption, authority, positional power and even experience in a field will lose importance.

However, AI won't have the ability to motivate, inspire and engage the workforce. Inspirational, rather than tactical, leadership is what will stimulate the workforce and industries of the future.

2. FROM IQ TO A NEW EQ

As previously noted, studies have suggested that personality traits, such as curiosity and emotional stability, will become twice as important to leadership as IQ.

Technology will take over many traditional leadership attributes. Reasoning with facts, data and figures, which are so important in the analysis and interpretation of complex data, means AI will be able to make predictions about future product and financial success. Leaders, therefore, will be required to focus more on their emotional stability or EQ. Persuasion, social understanding, humility and empathy must come to the fore.

"The future leader has to be more seat-of-pants driven, but they also have to have a very clear vision of what we described as, 'What does this convergence mean to me?' You know, 'Does it mean that I have to have clear values of how I want to lead the society?' Because that's what we're really talking about, right? We're talking about wealth generation, we're talking about the society in general. But then it's also diluted by the fact that this is not completely in my control. Today, the people who really control this world are people like Facebook. They have so much information, they have so much data, they probably know more about Nissan employees than Nissan does.

"So, even the ability to influence my employees is now shared with an outside industry – social media/internet. They have a lot of reach and influence on my employees than internal communications as in the past. Now, it's a reality. I may not like it, but it's a fact and how am I going to handle these issues and how am I going to cope with this? How am I going to keep my team motivated and how am I going to manage the speed? Attrition today is not a word that is relevant like it was 10 years back, it's a completely different word. It means very different things today. So, you're at two different ends here. Fifteen years back, I did skip level meetings. I did general assemblies. I had a company newsletter and I managed my employees. I told them what I needed to tell them and they were blissfully unaware of anything else.

"How do I get a Millennial to come and work in my company and specialize? Specialization was a word that was conceived 20 years back when people came and said, 'Look,

I'm a specialized hydraulic engineer.' Now, can there be a specialized hydraulic engineer? Especially as technologies are converging – something to think about. But, at the same time, it's not that specialisation is not relevant – it is the speed of technology evolution and the convergence of technology.

"Today, my employees probably know more about my company from every single article that's published anywhere in the world. So, my ability to influence them is equally a challenge. Employees are far more influenced by the articles they read online, in analysts' publications, social media, what they have been forwarded on WhatsApp and what they've got through Instagram and newspaper articles that get sent to their inbox every day. So, my employees are no longer singularly dependent on me for communicating with them but, more importantly, my ability to influence them.

"So, therefore, the demands of leadership are completely different to what they used to be. It's completely changed to EQ and agility. Previously, if you had an IQ of 160, you were well educated, you did an MBA, you started off in the right company, you would be successful. No doubt about it. Today, it is all about EQ and agility. This is the future requirement of leadership."

Kalyana Sivagnanam
President, Nissan Motor Corporation, and Regional Vice
President for Africa, Middle East and India
United Arab Emirates

PART 6

"There was a conversation piece about two weeks ago that we had, stimulated by Jack Ma's interview. He said don't teach people to do things that computers can do better. Because if you're teaching your kid to be an accountant, if you're sending him to school or university to be an accountant, chances are there will be a software program or computer built that will actually perfect it and do it a lot better than humans.

"Maybe in his prime, he might be able to match up to the computer but thereafter, the computer will outpace him. Our thinking, especially as a business that prides itself on intellectual property, is to teach creativity in the workplace. Business generally talks to IQ and EQ. An element that we also measure is AQ, which is the adaptability quotient of people to deal with high degrees or high levels of stress and high levels of pressure in the organization, especially being a service-based business. One of the critical things that we are actively pushing in our business is teaching people how to cope with levels of pressure, especially where there's an emotional contract between you and a client.

"In addition, a big focal point for us is teaching our employees the human element – the human-centricity of what we offer as a value proposition and as a product to our clients. Although we're a services business, whether you look at banking, insurance, the pension advisory, the pension fund market, the healthcare market ... I mean, if you look at the financial services system in South Africa, it's just over 14 trillion rand. It's about three times the country's GDP. We have less than 48% participation, formal participation, actively across those different disciplines. The question is, what is not happening in that market for there to be such a low level of participation? The answer to this is human-centricity. We have not been able to touch the 'Gogo/Grandmother' who operates out of her townhouse shop out in Soweto, who sells bread and milk to the local community. We have not been able to touch and inspire this community to actually use the bank as a trusted source to put their money into. And so, one of the big things that we're teaching our staff to do is build a sense of trust between you and your clients. How do you build human-centricity between you and your clients? Because a computer would never be able to replace this relationship."

Anthony Govender
CEO, ASI Financial Services
South Africa

3. FROM EGO TO HUMILITY

Leadership based on ego, power and directive authority is no longer relevant. It may achieve short-term successes, but the workforce of the future – the younger generation of today – will not accept this type of leadership. Leaders must put their egos aside and focus on helping and nurturing their teams for the benefit of the business, industry and society.

PART 6

"One thing that's interesting to me about this up-and-coming new generation of Millennials and digital natives, and all the terms we use to describe them, is this idea that I'm not locked into a job.

"All the data says that my daughter, who's 23, is likely to have 10 jobs or 15 jobs before she retires, and with lots of different organizations. If there's a whole generation of people coming into the workforce with that mentality, I think that's really exciting, actually, because it shows a level of freedom that previous generations have lacked. I think leading that generation will be really challenging, so a big challenge for leaders of the generation behind ours is, 'How am I going to lead?'

"The only way to lead a generation like that is through inspiration, because you have a whole generation who essentially assumes, 'I'll do this job for as long as it's interesting and I'm learning something new, and then I'll go find a new job. How long I stay and contribute to any one business or organization will depend entirely on how inspired they make me feel.' That, to me, is a really interesting leadership challenge. In a way, it's much more of a free market for labor than what it's been in the past.

"And in this war for talent and all the terms we use, if talented people have infinite choice, why should they pick you? What do you have to offer them that is different or better from what they could be offered somewhere else?

"Just think about the human potential you could unlock if you could really inspire people whose reason to go to work is, 'Inspire me and teach me something I don't know. That's why I go to work every day, not because of the pay cheque.' I think it changes the whole traditional system in a way that, over time, is really constructive."

David Everhart
Senior Vice President, Leaders and Talents, Mannaz A/S
London, United Kingdom

THE TRANSFORMATIONAL LEADER: DEVELOPING A COMPETITIVE ADVANTAGE

How do we build a competitive advantage and future proof our businesses? Unlocking the talent of the workforce of the future is critical. People want to be inspired, and they want to have a reason to go to work beyond a pay cheque. Our employees value a creative and innovative environment where their contribution makes a real difference. The workers of the future will care about the planet and its people. And they will insist their leaders share the same values.

As leaders, we need to inspire, motivate and engage people and teams. Our world is undergoing unprecedented change, and the only option is to grow and use this change as an opportunity instead of perceiving it as a threat.

Automation will play an ever-increasing role in our lives. Some say it makes our lives more complex and unpredictable and far less private. However, I believe cognitive technologies and artificial intelligence will add untold value to our lives – if we use them responsibly.

Apple Maps and Google Maps are great examples of cognitive technologies we now take for granted. Who still drives with a physical map to get to a location? Imagine how difficult that would be! You would definitely need a navigator in the car with you! Most people have embraced vehicle web-mapping services as everyday tools. They are cognitive technologies we would struggle to do without. And we see this as a positive contribution. Why would this not be the case for other cognitive and AI technologies?

As leaders, we need to stop sitting on the "technology fence". We need to get connected, involved and invested. If not, technology will become an existential threat at a scale we do not even understand today.

Leaders need to take the first step. Truly transformative leaders will unlock the potential and capabilities of their people because it's the people in our organizations who will create a new technology future. Great leaders identify talent and turn it into a powerful and creative force. It is this creative force that will future proof our businesses, our industries, our community and our world.

Transformational leaders share the following skills, competencies and characteristics:

1. They can unlock innovation and creativity in their companies. These leaders are agile, naturally curious and embrace design and critical thinking.
2. They realize the importance of effective coaching, mentoring and constructive feedback. They place a premium on leadership in their organization, excelling in developing their people.
3. They understand the importance of team effectiveness. They never compromise trust and integrity, and they embrace the notion that "great relationships make for great business".
4. They are mindful and inspirational. They are present and lead from the heart, not their ego. Mindful and inspirational leaders lead from a place of humility instead of a position of power.
5. They are master storytellers. They tell powerful stories that educate, motivate and change lives. They know that storytelling is an irresistible and powerful, strategic tool for change.

6. They actively build a competency around deep listening skills. Empathy, compassion and a real sense of caring are enhanced by their ability to truly listen.
7. They recognize that emotional intelligence is perhaps the most important factor in leading a fulfilled life. Compared to IQ, it is a better predictor of academic success, job performance and overall life success.

TRANSFORMATIONAL LEADERSHIP IMPACT

Transformational leaders lead by example. They lead from the front and encourage, inspire and motivate followers towards their vision. These leaders challenge employees to go beyond the ordinary, to create an aspirational future, one that once may have seemed impossible.

	What we were	What we are		What is required
Know self	Skepticism ✗	Confidence	and	Humility ✓
Lead self	Passive ✗	Action	and	Reflection ✓
Lead team	Reviews ✗	Results	and	Behaviors ✓
Lead business	Fragmented ✗	Core	and	Future ✓
Lead industry	Me ✗	Us	and	All ✓